THE OFFICIAL COMPANION BOOK

GLADIATORS

READY!

BLOOMSBURY PUBLISHING
LONDON • OXFORD • NEW YORK • NEW DELHI • SYDNEY

CONTENTS

INTRODUC

On one cold Saturday teatime in January 2024, a television programme exploded onto our screens in a blaze of glory. Millions of people crowded around their screens to watch one of the most amazing, action-packed, funny and heartfelt shows this country had ever seen.

A group of brave contenders, all of them just regular people, travelled to Sheffield and entered themselves into an almost-impossible challenge: to overcome sixteen elite athletes in a range of events that promised to test their strength, speed and determination to the absolute limit. Heroes would be made. Villains would be found. Every one of them would become superstars along the way. This is the power of Gladiators.

It immediately made a huge impact. The first episode of Gladiators 2024 was the biggest launch of a new entertainment show on the BBC for seven whole years; nearly ten million people watched the first episode. It was a big hit with families, in particular: four out of five of all 0–6-year-olds watched it. Clearly, there is something here for everyone.

For younger viewers, the Gladiators are real-life superheroes who look cool and fear nothing. But for the older viewers, there's a little nostalgia, too. Scores of parents grew up watching the 1990s version of Gladiators, idolising the likes of Hunter, Jet and Wolf. For these men and women, Gladiators represents a direct route back to their childhood. The show was able to bring families together as one. It's nothing

TION

'Heroes would be made. Villains would be found. Every one of them would become superstars along the way.'

short of remarkable to think that a group of athletes in sparkly Lycra and safety harnesses could have this effect.

If by some miracle you haven't enjoyed *Gladiators* yet, here is the show in a nutshell. Every episode, four contenders (two male and two female) take part in a

number of spectacular, dangerous, action-filled events. That alone would be enough to put most people off, but that isn't all. Standing in the way of the contenders are the Gladiators: sixteen giant, muscle-bound roadblocks whose mission is simple. The Gladiators exist to make the lives of the contenders as hard as possible.

Their role varies from event to event. In Duel, the Gladiators hit the contenders. In The Wall, they chase them. In Gauntlet, they line up in a row and slam into the contenders. As the events progress, the Gladiators charge at the contenders. They swing at them. They chase, tackle and bash them. It never lets up.

But this isn't the end. Once the Gladiators have sapped the contenders of all their

energy, it's time for the iconic Eliminator. This is the event where contender faces contender, in the ultimate obstacle course. They throw themselves over and under bars, climb ropes, balance on beams and finally face the dreaded Travelator – an uphill treadmill that can only be conquered if you sprint at it at top speed. Only the very best make it through to the next round. And only the best of the best emerges as the ultimate *Gladiators* champion.

However, don't think that the Gladiators are all just snarl and muscle. These sixteen figures all have distinct personalities, and they each approach the events differently. Maybe you can see yourself in some of them. If you're upbeat and positive, you might be able to identify with Nitro. If you're laid-back and relaxed, maybe you

can connect with Steel. If you're fierce and determined, you're probably a Sabre. If you happen to be completely in love with yourself to a truly disgusting degree, you're definitely a Legend.

But what makes a Gladiator? First, as you will soon see for yourself, it takes huge amounts of grit and determination. Every Gladiator has worked incredibly hard all their life to get to this point. They've trained long hours to become the very best in their field, sometimes conquering enormous odds to get there.

Some have powered through terrible injuries, or difficulties during childhood. Athena smashed the stereotypes to become one of the first champion female South Asian powerlifters. Fury was born

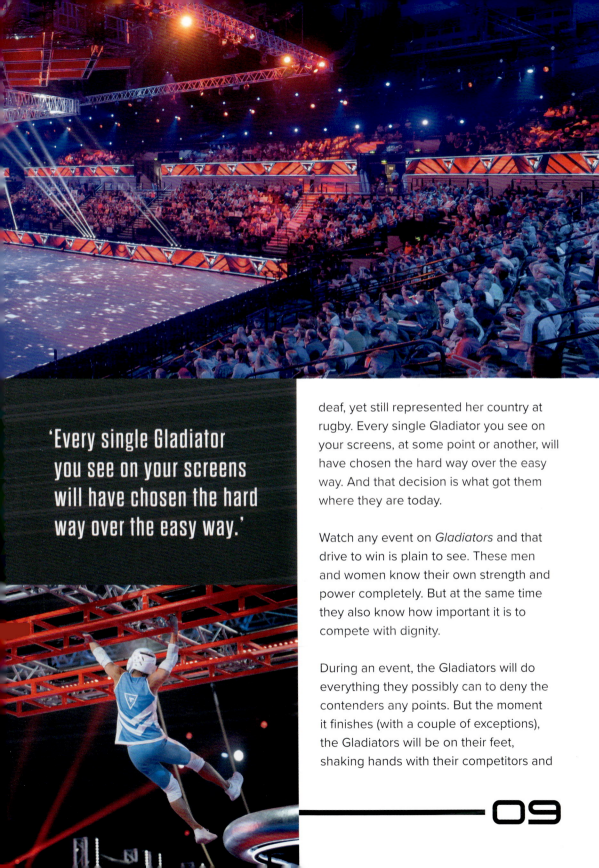

'Every single Gladiator you see on your screens will have chosen the hard way over the easy way.'

deaf, yet still represented her country at rugby. Every single Gladiator you see on your screens, at some point or another, will have chosen the hard way over the easy way. And that decision is what got them where they are today.

Watch any event on *Gladiators* and that drive to win is plain to see. These men and women know their own strength and power completely. But at the same time they also know how important it is to compete with dignity.

During an event, the Gladiators will do everything they possibly can to deny the contenders any points. But the moment it finishes (with a couple of exceptions), the Gladiators will be on their feet, shaking hands with their competitors and congratulating them for a game well fought. This is what makes them such great role models. They're gracious in victory, but they're also gracious in defeat.

Although there was that time Viper lost an event and then tried to eat Bradley Walsh's microphone, but maybe let's not dwell on that!

This spirit of fair play also extends to the relationships between the Gladiators themselves. They are a group of sixteen highly driven and competitive athletes who are the best at what they do. As such, you'd expect their group to be riddled with rivalry and ego. But that isn't the case at all. Speak to any of the Gladiators and they'll tell you how quickly they all bonded, and how they see themselves as a family.

And they really are. When one of the Gladiators wins, the others crowd around and celebrate. If one of them loses, they form into a huddle and try to boost them over the bump. The 2024 series saw its fair share of injuries, and there's a sense that all the Gladiators felt the pain as one. It's an unbelievably tight-knit group.

This is what makes them such an unstoppable force. When you face the Gladiators, you face an unbreakable, sixteen-strong unit. You face phantoms, giants, diamonds and legends. Every one

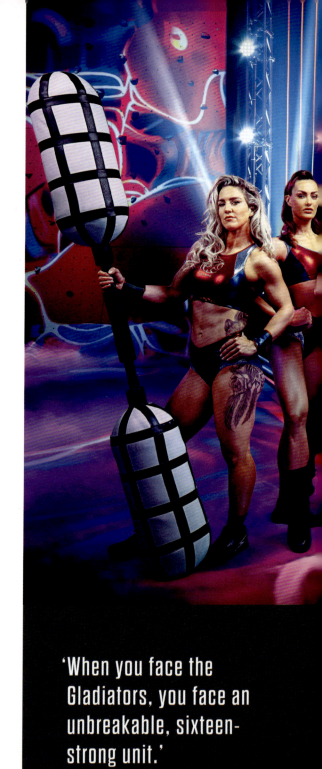

'When you face the Gladiators, you face an unbreakable, sixteen-strong unit.'

of them has been waiting their entire life to stop you. Do you feel their power? Do you have the will and the skill? Do you have the speed, the strength and the heart to be a winner?

Of course you do. GLADIATORS, READY?

MEET THE GLADIATOR

STATS

HEIGHT: **6 ft 5 in**
EATS: **6,400 cals/day**
CHEST: **133cm**

'The contenders all have a plan to beat me,
but as soon as I hit them with a pugil stick,
I guarantee that plan goes straight out the window.'

GIANT

INTRODUCING GIANT

Giant is called Giant for a reason. A former bodybuilder, he is a towering brick wall of a man, with biceps the size of American footballs, 73cm thighs and the same wingspan as an ostrich.

It's no wonder he excels at Duel – he ended *Gladiators* 2024 undefeated on it, and even knocked one poor contender off the podium in less than two seconds.

So, with this in mind, it's a surprise to learn just how gentle Giant is. He's kind, thoughtful, and wants everyone to feel included in whatever he does.

Part of his philosophy is to show his vulnerability, to make other people feel secure in their own weaknesses. Unfortunately for contenders, when it comes to the *Gladiators* events, his weaknesses are few and far between.

ABOUT ME

The Giant way
Be a nice guy. Be very, very competitive but also gracious in defeat, if that were ever to happen!

My workout routine
I go to the gym and train weights five times a week, and now I'm a Gladiator I'll attach a bit of climbing or functional agility to improve my cardio. Sometimes that means playing football with my son, or going for a bike ride with my wife, or hiking with my friends. Cardio is so boring that I try to make it enjoyable by doing it with people I like.

What I eat
In the morning, I eat a giant salad bowl full of porridge, with raisins, banana, honey, whey protein powder and a massive spoonful of almond butter. For lunch, I always have chicken, banana and cinnamon bagels. You cook a chicken breast, sprinkle a bit of cinnamon on, put a banana on the top, and then spread both sides of the bagel with nut butter. I know it sounds weird, but don't knock it until you've tried it. I eat four of them every day for lunch.

Growing up
I was always quite popular at school, and had a good circle of friends. I loved to be sporty and athletic, doing everything from football to badminton to athletics. I was a county shot putter, but my favourite sport as a youngster was football. I played for two football teams, so four days of the week I'd be playing football.

What I'm like in real life
I used to be a police officer, but I gave it up because the job wasn't what it looked like on TV. I thought there'd be a lot of car chases and running after people, but it's mainly paperwork. So I decided to become a firefighter instead. That was much better, and it suited my bodybuilding more. I could spend the time between call-outs weight training and eating properly. It was a complete win-win for me. Plus, in 2013, I posed for a firefighter calendar with Lee Phillips, who's now our Assistant Referee!

My favourite event on *Gladiators* ...
Obviously Duel. It's an individual sport. You're there by yourself, and it's one-on-one. All eyes are on you, and there's

the pressure of being expected to win. In *Gladiators* 2024 I had seven wins and zero defeats so, yeah, I did quite well.

... and my least favourite

I have an extreme fear of heights, so I hate The Edge. But I'm lucky, in a way. When we were all training before the show started, Damian, who oversees the rigging of the events in the arena, asked how much I weigh. I told him 130kg, and he said, 'Oh no, you're too heavy to do this event.' So I didn't even have to practise it, let alone do it!

My journey

The defining point in my life came when I was twenty-three. I was playing football and bodybuilding at the same time, but I had to choose between the two. I was a pretty good footballer, but I was never going to be professional. So, I thought I'd go all-in on bodybuilding and give it the best bash I could. I missed the team camaraderie of football, but I started winning medals as a bodybuilder, and everything snowballed from there.

My hero

David Beckham. Aside from all his sporting accomplishments, he's a family man. He has had to deal with a lot of media pressure, but he seems to handle it very well. He's been in the limelight for decades, but he's never pushed himself

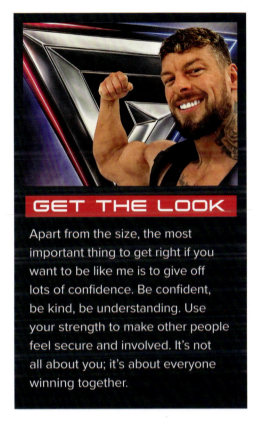

GET THE LOOK

Apart from the size, the most important thing to get right if you want to be like me is to give off lots of confidence. Be confident, be kind, be understanding. Use your strength to make other people feel secure and involved. It's not all about you; it's about everyone winning together.

in anyone's face. I really respect the qualities he shows.

What I've learned

As a Gladiator I'm a role model to millions of children and I take that responsibility very seriously. I want to make sure I am the best version of myself that I can be. It's important to try as hard as I can, but it's just as important to be friendly, approachable and to look out for others, whether that's my fellow Gladiators or the contenders.

THE WALL

HOW IT WORKS

One of the classic *Gladiators* events, The Wall gives the contenders one minute to scale a tricky ten-metre-high climbing wall. But here's the catch: soon after they set off, two hulking great Gladiators will be hot on their heels. Their sole aim is to catch the contenders and rip them from the wall as efficiently as possible before they reach the top. It's a high-risk event for everyone involved. Yes, the contenders are being pursued by elite athletes. But for the Gladiators, the potential for public failure is just as high. Just ask Diamond. In the 2024 series, she lunged for a contender's feet, only to fall away from the wall holding her shoe.

BASICS

TIME LIMIT:	**60** secs
GLADIATORS:	**2**
CONTENDERS:	**2**
WEAPONS:	**None**

SCORING

WINNER: **10** POINTS

SECOND OR STILL ON WALL WHEN TIME IS UP: **5** POINTS

FAILURE: **0** POINTS

'The Wall is a high-risk event for everyone involved.'

RULES

The Gladiators must only chase their assigned contender.

A successful climb is when the contender has both their feet over the wall.

Contenders may shake but not kick the Gladiators to dislodge them if they are grabbed over the course of the event.

SKILLS

SPEED: ▽ ▽ ▽ ▽ ▽

STRENGTH: ▽ ▽ ▽ ▽ ▽

AGILITY: ▽ ▽ ▽ ▽ ▽

BRAVERY: ▽ ▽ ▽ ▽ ▽

POWERBALL

HOW IT WORKS

If a contender has annoyed the Gladiators in a previous event, Powerball is where they'll seek their revenge. A frantic contact game requiring agility and speed, the contenders have to get more balls into scoring pods than their opponent. To complicate things, three hulking Gladiators stand in their way. To get on the scoring board at all, contenders need to sprint, dodge, weave ... and brace themselves for all kinds of crunching takedowns.

BASICS

TIME LIMIT: **60** secs
GLADIATORS: **3**
CONTENDERS: **2**
WEAPONS: **None**

SCORING

FOR EVERY BALL IN THE CENTRE POD: **3** POINTS
FOR EVERY BALL IN THE OUTER PODS: **2** POINTS

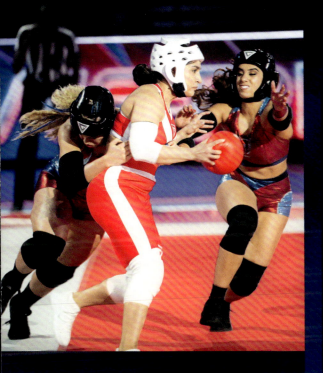

'Contenders need to sprint, dodge, weave ... and brace themselves for crunching takedowns.'

The contender may only carry one ball at any given time.

The Gladiator may prevent the contenders from scoring by blocking them, stripping the ball away, forcing the contender out of bounds or by tackling.

If a contender is tackled by a Gladiator and held for three seconds or is pulled down and the ball touches the ground, the Gladiator must release the contender immediately and the ball is considered dead.

SKILLS

SPEED: ▽ ▽ ▽ ▽ ▽

STRENGTH: ▽ ▽ ▽ ▽ ▽

AGILITY: ▽ ▽ ▽ ▽ ▽

BRAVERY: ▽ ▽ ▽ ▽ ▽

DUEL

HOW IT WORKS

Close your eyes and think of *Gladiators*, and chances are this is what you'll see. Two three-metre platforms, thirty centimetres apart from each other. A pair of two-metre-long pugil sticks. One snarling Gladiator raining down blow after colossal blow onto a quaking contender. Duel is *Gladiators* at its most elemental and arguably its most terrifying. The event only lasts for a maximum of thirty seconds, but just ask the contenders – it can feel like a lifetime up there.

BASICS

TIME LIMIT: **30** secs
GLADIATORS: **1**
CONTENDERS: **1**
WEAPONS: **Pugil stick**

SCORING

FOR A WIN: **10** POINTS
FOR A DRAW: **5** POINTS
FOR A LOSS: **0** POINTS

'Duel is *Gladiators* at its most elemental and arguably its most terrifying.'

The contender must try to knock the Gladiator off the opposite platform while trying to prevent being knocked off their own.

The Duel ends when either the contender or the Gladiator is knocked from their platform.

Only the pugil stick must be used. No jabbing, pushing, shoving, kicking or use of hands or legs is allowed.

SKILLS

SPEED: ▽ ▽ ▽ ▽ ▽

STRENGTH: ▽ ▽ ▽ ▽ ▽

ABILITY: ▽ ▽ ▽ ▽ ▽

BRAVERY: ▽ ▽ ▽ ▽ ▽

MEET THE GLADIATOR

STATS

HEIGHT: **5 ft 8 in**

ARM LENGTH: **58cm**

KEY SKILL: **Flexibility**

'I'm not afraid of anything.
Except spiders.'

INTRODUCING COMET

DID YOU KNOW?

Comet used to be a 10-metre platform diver.

LONGEST-HELD HANDSTAND

over 2 minutes
(168 seconds)

MAXIMUM BACKFLIPS IN A ROW

10
(this is a lot)

Comet had the fewest appearances of any Gladiators in the 2024 series, thanks to a critical ankle injury that she sustained after an unlucky fall on Hang Tough. But this just means that viewers will have more surprises in store when they see her in 2025.

As an ex-gymnast and cheerleader, Comet has spent her entire life flipping herself upside-down and throwing herself about. This has made her fast, flexible and tough – in other words, a complete nightmare for contenders.

Don't be fooled by her elegance. Comet means business, and her relentless self-belief means that she never, ever gives up.

ABOUT ME

The Comet way
Smiley, feminine, strong and fearless.

My workout routine
Twice a day, six times a week. In the morning I'll do strength training, alternating my days been legs and upper body. But since *Gladiators*, the training has been more tailored towards specific events. Now I do a lot of functional training (squats, lunges, push and pull movements, etc.), plus climbing and gymnastics. Sundays are my rest day, but I'll always go on a long walk to stay active.

What I eat
I am a chocoholic! I eat chocolate every day. But it's important to make sure you fuel your body correctly for the training you do and for the muscle mass that you have, so my diet is pretty high protein, with carbs when I am training and little treats here and there. I eat a lot. Most of us do, especially Giant. He eats loads!

Growing up
I was a bit of a goody-two-shoes when I was younger. I liked to chat a bit too much, but I actually did pretty well at school. I was very creative and excelled at sport and art. I had a really nice group of friends. In fact, I have no bad memories of school at all; I loved it.

What I'm like in real life
I started gymnastics when I was five. I was just obsessed. By the time I was seven, I was training four hours a day, four times a week. It was intense, but it got me to county competitions, then regional, and then international. But by the time I was thirteen, I had physically grown so much that it was too demanding on my body, so I got into diving. I remember seeing Tom Daley on the TV, and I knew that was the sport for me. I went off to train in America and I would have stayed there, but I missed my family too much. And then when I started uni, I joined the cheer squad. That involved lots of tumbling, jumping and stunting, and I loved it so much that I thought about becoming a stuntwoman. I'm pretty fearless.

My favourite event on *Gladiators* ...
Hang Tough. Even though I got injured after playing it, I still love it. I'm a gymnast, so I'm not scared of heights. When I'm up there, I don't just want

to win – I want my legs to be straight and my toes to be pointed. Gymnastics requires perfection, so I like my performance to look pristine.

... and my least favourite

The Ring or Powerball. Contact sports are not my skill set. But we're Gladiators, so we're not afraid to get stuck into anything.

My journey

On my third recording, I broke my ankle after landing awkwardly after Hang Tough. I had surgery, and now I have two plates and ten screws in my foot. It was five or six months before I could walk fully again. I'm not going to lie, it was hard. I still went to the arena every day to support the rest of the team, but it really wasn't easy seeing everyone out there competing while I had to wait backstage. But I've worked hard to recover to full fitness, and next series is mine for the taking. I'm ready!

My hero

My mum Is Superwoman. I lost my dad when I was fourteen, and Mum put everything on hold to give me and my brother the life that we have. She put us into the sports that we wanted to do, made sure we were at training on time. If I can be like her when I'm older, I'll be the happiest person ever.

GET THE LOOK

To be like me you need to have composure and be graceful and elegant – and smile! You need to have self-belief and be strong, too. I want to show people that you can look the way you want to look, and prove that you can have muscles and still be feminine.

What I've learned

My injury taught me that mentally I am extremely tough and resilient. I think whatever happens in life, no matter if it's injury-based or not, the way you respond to situations is everything. You can sit and feel sorry for yourself, or you can think, 'Do you know what? I can come back from this.' Self-belief is such a massive thing.

THE GLADIATOR MINDSET

You need many things to be a Gladiator, such as speed, agility and strength. More than anything, though, you need the right mindset. You need to learn to *think* like a Gladiator.

In theory, this sounds easy, because on the surface it seems to involve thinking the word 'Grrr' a lot. But dig a little deeper and you'll see that all the Gladiators possess an incredible amount of focus and determination. If you spend any time with any of them, it's almost guaranteed that before long, one of them will say, 'Shoot for the moon, because even if you miss you'll be among the stars.' And you won't correct them by pointing out that actually the stars are a lot further away than the moon either, because they're Gladiators and you're not.

Regardless, here are the top tips to gaining the all-important Gladiator mindset.

Visualisation

Almost all the Gladiators practise visualisation, a sports psychology technique where you mentally rehearse your performance over and over again before it begins, until it settles into your mind and becomes second nature. 'I think a lot of athletes use this technique,' explains Athena. 'It's about picturing yourself succeeding beforehand. Sometimes events can be daunting, and it can be scary not knowing what to expect. But it's about being your own champion, and removing any edge of doubt that you might have.'

'I take a very realistic approach to my visualisation,' adds Sabre. 'I'm honest with myself about what's going to be difficult, and the areas of that event where my strengths lie. It reminds me that I need to try a lot harder, and that I really need to concentrate.'

Some Gladiators visualise more than other, however. Some of them will just think about the event itself. Not Steel, though. He got where he is by thinking much further into the future. 'Say I'm about to do The Wall,' he says. 'I'll visualise the whole thing. Climbing the wall. Taking the contender down. How I'm going to celebrate. And then I'll even visualise talking to Bradley and Barney afterwards.'

'The one thing that has really helped me is just acting like I'm confident, even if I'm not.'
FURY

Stay in the moment

Of course, visualisation might work for some people. But for those of us who have a habit of overanalysing things, it can also be a shortcut to overwhelm. By her own admission, Fire is a monumental overanalyser, and her recipe to combat this is to stay in the moment. If visualising means looking to the future, then she would much prefer to remain firmly in the present.

'I stay in the moment, rather than think ahead,' she explains. 'Listen, before the ref says, "Gladiators, ready," nothing matters. I used to be a sprinter, a sport where the warm-up took two hours, and the actual race took less than eleven seconds. You have to stop yourself from getting in your head. Remove the uncontrollable factors. Before an event, the only thing you need to worry about is the next minute.'

Self-belief

Another thing the Gladiators have in common is a world-beating, potentially quite scary, sense of confidence. They know how strong they are; how incredible they look; and how many contenders they'll crush along the way. 'Some of us just want to be the best,' Apollo says. 'If it's me versus you, then it's gonna be me. We're supposed to be the epitome of excellence.

We wouldn't be here if we were constantly giving in to doubt.'

Nor should self-belief be misconstrued as arrogance. 'It's all well and good thinking you're better than everyone else,' continues Apollo. 'But have you actually got the proof? I have. I know all the blood, sweat and tears that it took to get me here. When I'm standing in front of a contender, I can look myself in the eye and say without a doubt that I am who I say I am. Can they?'

Do the things that scare you

Not everyone has Apollo's bulletproof swagger, but that doesn't matter. You wouldn't know it to see her growling at you in the arena, but as a child Fury struggled with crippling shyness. And this only started to go away when she discovered an important tool: fake it till you make it.

'The one thing that has really helped me is just acting like I'm confident, even if I'm not,' she says. 'I'm not cocky, but I just try to act like I belong, wherever I am.' And the way to do this is to push yourself into situations that scare your pants off. 'Whenever you think, "I can't do this, I'm too nervous," you just push yourself to do it anyway,' she suggests. 'Because afterwards you will feel so much better for doing it. Even if you

don't feel it in the heat of the moment, I promise that you'll feel great afterwards.'

Zone in

In the moments before any event, a lot of the Gladiators will take themselves away to be on their own for a few minutes, to help them focus better on the task at hand. Even Phantom, who makes a point of blasting top-volume Girls Aloud songs while he warms up, will grab a moment of solitude before he walks out into the arena. 'Yeah, I spend five minutes getting into the zone beforehand,' he says. 'I need the tunnel vision. If you've got a task to do, it's important to take some time to make sure you're doing it properly. If you can't focus your mind for five minutes, then I don't know if you should be a Gladiator.'

Psychological warfare

Obviously, tunnel vision doesn't just benefit you. Sometimes you can use it as a tool to freak out the contenders who you're about to face in an event. Enter Bionic, the undisputed king of psychological warfare.

'Just before an event, I'll walk around and stare them down a little bit, just to get in their heads,' he smiles. 'Whether it's cruel or not I don't know, but at the end of the day, we're there to do a job.'

Does it work? 'Sometimes you can see the fear in the contender's face, but it depends on their personality,' he says. 'I'll decide whether I want to speak to them or just stare at them silently. Whatever will throw them off more, that's what I'll do.'

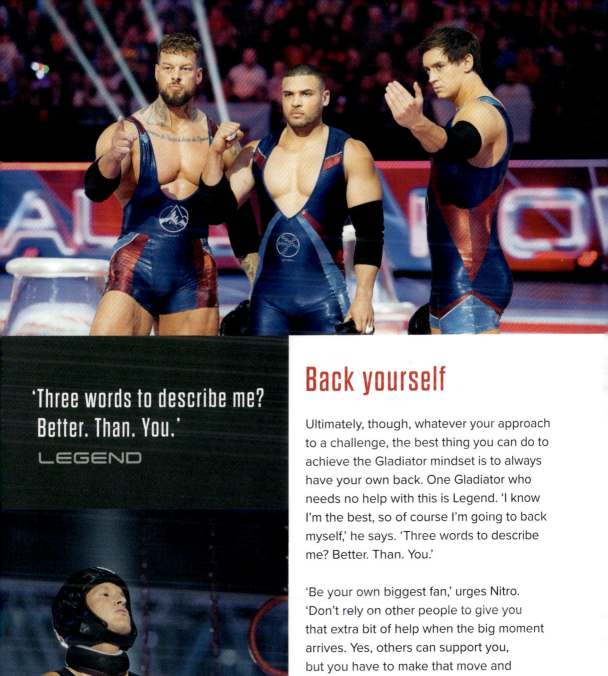

Back yourself

Ultimately, though, whatever your approach to a challenge, the best thing you can do to achieve the Gladiator mindset is to always have your own back. One Gladiator who needs no help with this is Legend. 'I know I'm the best, so of course I'm going to back myself,' he says. 'Three words to describe me? Better. Than. You.'

'Be your own biggest fan,' urges Nitro. 'Don't rely on other people to give you that extra bit of help when the big moment arrives. Yes, others can support you, but you have to make that move and take charge of the situation. Sure, these contenders are good. They might land a blow or two. But don't sweat it. Just remember, you are a Gladiator. You are the best of the best. That's all that matters.'

MEET THE GLADIATOR

STATS

HEIGHT: **6 ft 1 in***
THIGH: **66cm**
LOVES: **Himself**

'I feel sorry for the other Gladiators. It must be very hard to compete with me every day.'

*(although he claims 6 ft 9 in)

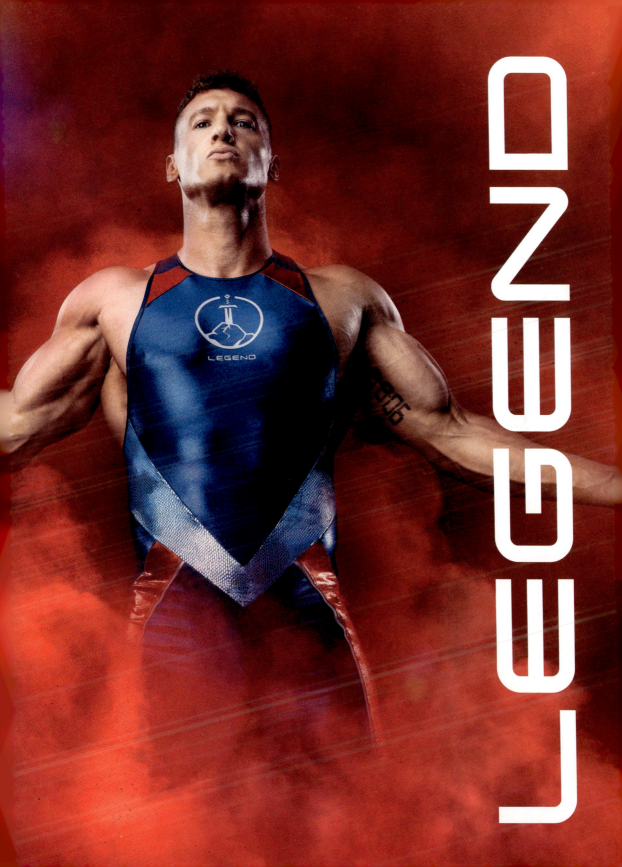

INTRODUCING LEGEND

DID YOU KNOW?

Legend says that Giant and Bionic are too muscly. 'It's too much, they both look ridiculous.'

MAXIMUM TRIPLE JUMP

15m 50cm
(longer than eight beds end to end)

MAXIMUM DEADLIFT

320kg
(heavier than three male pandas)

What can you say about Legend that he hasn't already repeatedly said himself?

Describing himself as a cross between Gandhi and David Hasselhoff, Legend is easily the most self-assured Gladiator around. Swaggering into events like a returning war hero, Legend's ego is so monumental that it can be seen from outer space.

Worse still, he has the skills to back it up. Unbeaten on Hang Tough and an eight-time competitor on The Edge, Legend also holds the record for knocking a contender off the Collision bridge in just three seconds.

What's more, he has a fiercely sharp wit, noting in a post-event interview that 'There is no "i" in "team", but there are five of them in "individual brilliance".'

So, fine, Legend is great. Just please don't tell him.

ABOUT ME

The Legend way

I set the bar very, very high. Very high. Typically, if you're doing a pole vault, you balance the bar high up on these little stands. But I set the bar so high that the stands can't even reach the bar. I have to make my own bespoke stands for my bar, because that's how high I set it.

My workout routine

Two times a day, six days a week. Gym in the morning, and then Gladiator training in the afternoon. So it's sprints, climbing, rugby. I just built a swimming pool at home, and guess what? I've put a Hang Tough rig over it.

What I eat

I eat everything, because I have a very fast metabolism. So it's a high-protein diet, and lots of fruit and veg, but then I just eat what I want. I eat burgers and pizzas, because if you only eat chicken, rice and broccoli all day, your life's going to be horrible.

Growing up

I was exactly the same. Try to imagine me now, but just a little bit smaller. That's what I was like at school. Still very much the best. I was the best in my class. I was the best in my school. I'm better now, but I was still the best back then, too.

What I'm like in real life

I am exactly the same as I am onscreen. I'm still great. I just transfer it to other things. If you see me in a supermarket doing my shopping, you'll notice that I happen to be an incredible shopper. If I'm looking for a certain type of product, I'll find it straight away. I can also carry an unbelievable amount of shopping. Supermarket employees frequently say to me, 'How are you carrying that much? I've never seen anyone do that.'

My favourite event on *Gladiators* ...

Hang Tough and The Wall, because I'm extremely good at them. Probably too good, in fact. I actively have to stop training for them, because the producers asked me to stop being so good.

... and my least favourite

My least favourite are the team events, because it means I have to be with other Gladiators. They bring me down. Imagine if you had Lionel Messi playing for a Sunday League team. He probably wouldn't enjoy that, because he's competing with players of a much lower calibre. Same for me and Powerball.

My journey

I was a PE teacher for five years before I was a Gladiator. People say that PE teachers have it easy, but I challenge anyone to take thirty fourteen-year-old kids out onto a playing field, and give them all javelins, and keep them all under control. The school I worked at had a really cool PE department, and naturally I was the greatest PE teacher ever. I was literally always graded as outstanding. So even as a teacher, I could still reach those lofty heights.

My hero

Myself, to be honest. I am my greatest role model. I'll often just look at clips of myself, that's my biggest inspiration. I'll just sit back and be like, 'Wow, that's good, mate. You're amazing.'

What I've learned

I've learned how much I inspire the other Gladiators. They'll probably tell you this, but they all took inspiration from me. I frequently see them across the room, looking at me and watching me and getting inspired.

GET THE LOOK

The first thing I would point out, straight off the bat, is that you can't really get my look. It isn't realistic. It's like me saying I want to be a sperm whale. It isn't going to happen, is it? But if you want to try to get my look, then first you need to be unbelievably attractive. Be handsome, have good hair, get a great skin tone, have a nice tan, be extremely muscular. And in terms of moves, just be low key. Some of the Gladiators have ridiculously intricate moves, and they're trying too hard. So just cross your arms, look at people and be cool. That's all.

DO THE MOVES 01

STEEL

 WALK-OUT MOVE

STEP 01 Come out with your arms outstretched, soaking up the applause.

STEP 02 Cross your arms, but bring one hand up to your chin. Look like you're thinking about something really hard.

STEP 03 Now smile.

ALTERNATIVE POSE

Hulk out — Flex your biceps and act like you're ripping an imaginary shirt.

'Kids are always coming up to me and trying to rip their shirts open these days.'

STEEL

SABRE WALK-OUT MOVE

'When I walk into the arena, I'm showing everyone how sweet and innocent I am ... then the claws come out.'

STEP 01 Walk out slowly, swaying your hips from side to side as you do.

STEP 02 Turn to the side, and run your hands up through your hair with your eyes closed.

STEP 03 Now drop into a lateral squat. Shift your weight to one side and bend that knee into a squat, while keeping the other leg straight.

STEP 04 Make your hands into claws. Pull one back to your ear and keep the other in front of you.

STEP 05 Walk forwards, then raise one knee and push an invisible opponent away from you with your hip.

 ALTERNATIVE POSE

Two claws – One stretched in front of you, the other curled up over your head like a scorpion's tail.

NITRO

'It's all about energy, confidence and vibes.'

WALK-OUT MOVE

STEP 01 Walk out full of energy, raising your hands to pump up the crowd.

STEP 02 Put one fist on top of the other, one potato two potato-style, and bang them together twice.

STEP 03 Twirl your index fingers around each other, like you're telling someone to wind up whatever they're doing.

STEP 04 Wind one hand around the top of your head, then point to the sky. Hold the pose.

STEP 05 Jump as high as you can, and land on the floor with a crash.

ALTERNATIVE POSE

Reach one arm up high, then bring it down and point at the audience.

VIPER

 WALK-OUT MOVE

STEP 01 Walk out slowly, glaring at everyone.

STEP 02 Bring your hands together. Raise one knee. Now bring your hands down on the raised knee, hard.

STEP 03 Bring one elbow out in front of you, like you're trying to hit something with it.

STEP 04 Now hit that elbow with your other hand and hold the pose.

STEP 05 Punch the ground with one hand. Look angry throughout.

 ALTERNATIVE POSE

'Smash!'

Viper does not need an alternative move. He is already terrifying enough.

FIRE

'When I walk out, I'm trying to blow the contenders away.'

WALK-OUT MOVE

STEP 01 Skip out with sass.

STEP 02 Stop, with a wide stance. Twist your body to the side and raise one arm until it's level with your face.

STEP 03 Turn to the other side, making a big wide circle with your arms, then bring your hands together. Pretend there's something in them that you don't want people to see.

STEP 04 Now throw an invisible fireball towards the audience as hard as you can.

STEP 05 Skip forward, stop, bend over and blow the fire towards everyone.

ALTERNATIVE POSE

Blast the audience with an invisible fireball.

FURY

'The first part of my walk-out move is actually British Sign Language. It means "furious".'

 WALK-OUT MOVE

STEP 01 Walk out angrily.

STEP 02 Drop to one knee.

STEP 03 Keeping your elbows bent, raise your hands to your face in a claw shape, while looking ferocious.

STEP 04 As you stand up, straighten your arms and pull them back behind you.

STEP 05 Quickly bring them forward and, with one hand, punch the palm of the other.

 ALTERNATIVE POSE

Just do the part where you angrily raise your hands.

LEGEND

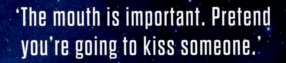

'The mouth is important. Pretend you're going to kiss someone.'

 ## WALK-OUT MOVE

STEP 01 Walk out with your head held high. Blow the audience a kiss, then raise your hands above your head to better absorb the crowd's love.

STEP 02 Point to the audience.

STEP 03 Stroke your beautiful, perfect face.

STEP 04 Fold your muscley, perfect arms.

STEP 05 Pout your perfectly perfect lips.

 ## ALTERNATIVE POSE

Just feel how soft and smooth your face is.

GIANT

> 'Make yourself as big as you can, that's my advice.'

 ## WALK-OUT MOVE

STEP 01 Walk out with your arms outstretched, to make you look as huge and as intimidating as possible.

STEP 02 With your arms still out, cross your hands in front of you.

STEP 03 Pull them back towards you and put your hands on your hips, making sure to puff your chest out and show off your lat (wing) muscles.

STEP 04 While pointing at the audience, flex your bicep on your other arm.

STEP 05 Now flex both of them together. You mean business.

 ## ALTERNATIVE POSE

Hands on hips, chin down, fierce scowl.

MEET THE GLADIATOR

STATS

HEIGHT: **5 ft 7 in**
BICEP: **34cm**
KEY SKILL: **Takedowns**

'People think I'm angry with them,
but I'm just in the zone!'

FURY

INTRODUCING FURY

Fury comes to *Gladiators* with a long list of accomplishments to her name. She played rugby for England. She's a former British jiu jitsu champion. She's won titles in the Deaf Athletics Championship, and she has repeatedly won the world coal-carrying championship, which involves running a mile with a 20kg sack of coal on your back.

By rights she should be as arrogant as Legend, yet you're unlikely to come across a nicer human being. The spirit of sportsmanship beats through Fury like a drum, which should be evident to any of the contenders that Fury has trounced in competition and then hugged.

ABOUT ME

The Fury way

I've got two personalities in me. There's competition mode, where I'm focused like a laser on that event. I want to win, I'm in the zone. I'm not there to make friends; I'm just there to smash my way to victory. But as soon as I hear the whistle, something switches and the other side of me comes out. I hug people, I congratulate them. It's all about sportsmanship.

My workout routine

I was a professional rugby player, so my workout routine is very mixed. I used to do strength, speed and rugby training and then playing on the weekend. But now it's very different because I have to train to be a Gladiator, so it's still a work in progress.

What I eat

I've never been very focused on calories or things like that. I just eat well, and then try to have a bit of balance on a weekend. By balance, I mean treats.

Growing up

I was really shy in school, but I threw myself into PE. Sports day was literally like the Olympics for me. I took it so seriously, it's actually embarrassing to think about it! But in terms of education and being at school, I was very, very shy and didn't have much confidence. Rugby helped to change things, because it's a team sport. I was forced to speak to people, and my confidence grew from there. You meet new people, go to new places. I can't recommend the sport enough to anyone, to be honest. The benefits you get from it are pretty amazing.

What I'm like in real life

I absolutely love rugby. But I've always had issues with confidence, doubting myself and thinking, 'I'm not good enough.' Bear in mind, I got my first England cap when I was eighteen, and I was travelling the world, but still thinking, 'Oh, I'm not as good as this other player.' When you're in an elite environment, you can't help compare yourself. But when I actually look back, I'm like, 'Oh, I must have done pretty well.' When you play for England, you know, you're competing for a shirt. You're always going against someone for that same spot on the team. But because you're on the same team, you also want to support each other. It's a bizarre environment to be in.

My favourite event on *Gladiators* ...
Oh, anything with contact. Physical contact. I love that. The one that surprised me most is The Edge. I knew I'd probably enjoy it, but I didn't think I'd enjoy it as much as I did. I love the chess element of it, figuring out where the contender's next move will be – and the adrenaline, running at such a height.

... and my least favourite
I didn't get a chance to try The Wall during the 2024 series. But if it comes up next time around, I'll get stuck in.

My journey
I was one of the youngest people in the UK to get a cochlear implant. I was fourteen months old. People think that when you get a cochlear implant they just switch it on and you can hear straight away, but it's a lot of work. My implant is visible on TV, and I don't think I really understood how big an impact that would have. From the first episode, the response I got from kids, parents and teachers has blown me away. Girls with cochlear implants are going into school with blue braids and getting into rugby. It's made me realise what a privileged position I'm in. I don't want to ever take that for granted.

My hero
It's mostly my family. My dad won multiple

GET THE LOOK

It's quite a bold look. When I thought warrior-type vibes, I thought that maybe I could have braids. But they're quite complicated. There are French braids and Viking braids, plus there's blue running through it, so it takes an hour and a half to do. But it's worth it.

titles in MMA [Mixed Martial Arts] and Brazilian jiu jitsu, so he had a big impact on me. My auntie as well. She was blind. So with my deafness we had quite a bit to bond over. She's no longer with us, but there are stories about her that even now change how I go about life.

What I've learned
I was very nervous going into *Gladiators*. The first time I saw the stage I thought, 'I'm not going to be able to walk out in front of everyone.' But I did, and I ended up really embracing it. The show has taught me that if I push myself, I've actually got more confidence than I think I have.

TEAMWORK MAKES THE DREAM WORK

On paper, the Gladiators make an unlikely team. Every one of them is an elite athlete who spent their entire life striving to be the best. They're all strong, single-minded and incredibly competitive. When they get together, there should be fireworks.

But that isn't the case. Ask any of the Gladiators, and they'll all happily tell you what a tight-knit bunch they are. They compete together onscreen, but they hang out away from the show and have a group WhatsApp chain that keeps their phones buzzing day and night. They really are a happy family.

This is as much of a surprise to the Gladiators themselves as it is to anyone else. 'Bringing sixteen people together, all from different backgrounds and different

sports, it doesn't mean that you are going to get along,' says Fury. 'There are big personalities. It's very easy to clash.' At first, this looked like it might be the case. When they met and trained for the first time, Apollo admits to spending the first few minutes sizing everyone up. 'When you put a bunch of competitive people in the same room, you're always going to compare yourself to everyone at first,' he says.

But that went away quickly, and (for the most part) the Gladiators now view themselves as a band of equals. 'When we all met each other, we all assumed that there would be a couple of Gladiators who'd be happier outside the main group, but there genuinely isn't,' says Sabre. 'Of course we're gonna be competitive with each other, but we're very supportive of

one another,' adds Electro. 'Everyone really does just get along. It's awesome to have that family behind you.'

So why have the Gladiators succeeded at forming a team against all odds?

Here are their main lessons:

They make each other better

One phrase the Gladiators use a lot is: 'Iron sharpens iron.' In other words, if you're surrounded by the best, your game is bound to improve. 'If one of the Gladiators has a great performance, my instinct is to go out there and beat it,' says Apollo. 'But it's all healthy competition. We all have that same collective mindset, where we all just keep pushing and pushing each other to improve. The 2024 series was great, but now we all know what we can do, so we're all pushing ourselves to be even tougher for 2025. We all want to be able to look back on this time and say that we really gave it our all. Being part of an elite team like this makes that easier to achieve.'

They know the value they bring

Any team is only as good as the personalities within it, and all the Gladiators know that they each have skills that help bring the group together. 'I'm a little older than some of the other Gladiators,' says Steel. 'That means if anyone has any issues with anything, they know they can always come to me for a chat. I definitely feel like the big brother of the group.'

Meanwhile, the youngest Gladiator Dynamite knows that she keeps the mood up. 'I'm never really serious,' she smiles. 'I'm always running around, or doing handstands, or trying to boss some of the bigger Gladiators around, which is funny because I'm so tiny. Basically, I just try to keep everyone young.'

Unless they're Legend

Actually, it might be a slight exaggeration to say that there are no egos in the group, because Legend is part of that Gladiator family.

When asked about his attitude to teamwork, he points out that he sees himself as 'the champion of the group'. He says he helps the Gladiators improve as a team because 'I do whatever I want, and the others all follow along behind me, wishing they were more like me. I'm a beacon of hope, the alpha male. When we eat together, I sit at the head of the table because everyone wants to look at me and be like me.'

If you say so, Legend!

'Everyone really does just get along. It's awesome to have that family behind you.'
ELECTRO

They put the group before the individual

The Gladiators know it's important to always put the group's interests first – even in the choice of music they listen to when they're getting ready. 'It's not about what you like, it's about what gets the energy right in the room,' explains Nitro. 'When I get the speakers out, I make sure we play music that everyone's into, not just me. The synergy, and what motivates the group, is something I give a lot of thought to. I think the experience wouldn't be the same if we were all out for ourselves.'

Fury agrees with this sentiment. 'People put a lot of effort in trying to get the right mix of personalities. We each bring something unique to the table. We all have different strengths and different weaknesses, so we can all help and balance each other out.'

They have a common goal

For the Gladiators, nothing bonds the team like having a shared target to focus on. Unfortunately for anyone who applies to go up against them, that focus is stopping the contenders. 'We all watch the contenders,' says Electro. 'And sometimes we'll huddle up and analyse their performances, so we have a better idea of how to beat them.'

And if a contender hurts a Gladiator, there can be hell to pay. 'In one round, Bionic injured himself against one particular contender,' says Phantom. 'The next event was Duel, and I faced him myself, and he lasted two seconds. I took the anguish of what happened to Bionic out on him, and I won.'

They remember the bigger picture

Very importantly, too, the Gladiators all know that they're part of a bigger system. 'Our team extends beyond the Gladiators,' Phantom says. 'The production staff and the crew behind the scenes are incredible. They all work so hard, from the physios who help keep us in good shape to the chefs who give me my cake for breakfast every morning. Even when they're tired, they all have great big smiles on their faces, because they're just as happy to be there as we are. Between us, we've created this bubble that just feels so special.'

MEET THE GLADIATOR

STATS

HEIGHT: **6 ft 6 in***
THIGH: **76cm**
KEY SKILL: **Strength**

'The contenders don't bother me,
I'm just there to win ... and get the job done!'

*(or 6 ft 9 in if you count the hair)

BIONIC

INTRODUCING BIONIC

DID YOU KNOW?

One of Bionic's favourite things to do when not training is to play football-management games on his laptop.

MAXIMUM LEG PRESS

700kg

(the same weight as a buffalo)

MAXIMUM DEADLIFT

320kg

(the same weight as fourteen full holiday suitcases)

Of all the Gladiators, Bionic might just be the hardest to miss. Joint-tallest with Apollo (although his bleach-blond flat-top hair gives him the edge), Bionic is a hulking mass of a man.

A former bodybuilder with 48cm biceps and size 13 feet, this is a Gladiator who completely understands how to use his size to his advantage. Undefeated in Duel and boasting more takedowns than any other male Gladiator in Collision, even an ankle injury sustained during Gauntlet didn't stop him in *Gladiators* 2024.

Now he's raring to go again, fitter than ever, and he has a point to prove. Contenders have every right to be nervous.

ABOUT ME

The Bionic way

No matter who I come up against, they're gonna go home on the losing side. No discussion. I'm unbeaten.

My workout routine

On a typical day, I'll train for up to two hours with weights, and do some cardio as well. As a Gladiator, I need to focus on my functional movement, because I'm a big guy. I've always been fast, but I'm trying to become more agile.

What I eat

When I was a bodybuilder, I was on 7,000 calories a day, which meant eating every three hours. I had to set alarms to wake myself through the night so I could eat. Now it's not as crazy because I am in more athletic shape to take part in *Gladiators*. I still eat six times a day, but the portions are nowhere near as big.

My school years

I had lots of friends growing up, but I was tragic at school. I didn't get on with the lessons at all. I got two GCSEs and was bottom set in most things. In Year Six I moved to Australia and had to take an entry test, but I did so badly that they moved me down a year. I moved back to the UK four years later and I found that I couldn't fit in properly. I struggled a lot, and I was getting picked on and stuff. Sport was my salvation.

What I'm like in real life

I got into bodybuilding when I was quite young, about seventeen years old. It's an individual sport, which requires so much focus that you think it's the most important thing in the world when you're doing it. *Gladiators* is the opposite of that, though. You still need focus and a positive mindset, but it's great to have a team around you. It's definitely changed me for the better.

My favourite event on *Gladiators* ...

There's nothing I don't like. I fancy myself against anyone, end of. If you come up against me, you're going to get hit hard, and it's your fault for signing up. Did you see me on Gauntlet? In one episode I flung a contender from the back of the course all the way to the front. People get hit. It's not a joke.

... and my least favourite

Least favourite? Me? Nah.

My journey

When I was sixteen, I was in a car accident. I broke most of my ribs and my ankle, and I punctured a lung. I was airlifted away, and I have no memory of it at all. For weeks afterwards I struggled to walk, so I was sent to rehab in a gym. And that's where I discovered weights, and that's what led me to bodybuilding and my love for working out.

My hero

Micah Richards. Not as a footballer, but as a pundit. He does things his way, and he doesn't care about how anyone else does it. He's the life and soul on a panel of pundits. He puts his own spin on things and has developed this whole new way of doing things.

What I've learned

I've always been very prone to injury. I don't do maximum-weight deadlifts at the gym, because I know I'll hurt my spine. But I injured my ankle badly on the previous series of *Gladiators,* playing Gauntlet. The contender was agile and was getting past me. As I turned to go after him, my ankle went. After resting for a couple of days, I could carry on in the series, and now it is much stronger. I'm looking forward to getting back to it, because I know what I'm capable of in that event.

GET THE LOOK

You need to get yourself a good hairdresser if you want to look like me. Find a hairdresser who has a lot of bleach, work non-stop at the gym, and be very tall. But the hair is really the most distinctive thing.

THE HISTORY LESSON

The Gladiators you see on TV are not the first gladiators. That title belongs to the Roman gladiators, who trained and fought nearly 2,000 years ago. In many ways their lives were much tougher, because defeat would mean certain death. But then again, The Edge hadn't been invented back then, so who knows.

The history of the Roman gladiators began back in the third century BCE. At first, they started as a funeral rite for wealthy Romans, who believed that bloodshed would honour the dead, so they started making people fight to the death during the ceremony. But as the Roman Empire grew, so did the scale of the events. Before long, entire amphitheatres were filled with tens of thousands of spectators, all roaring on the fighters.

And these were big shows, too. As well as fights, there would be parades, mock naval battles and extravagant animal hunts featuring rhinos, hippos, elephants, giraffes, lions, tigers and bears. Unfortunately, these were often just as bloodthirsty as the gladiator games.

Like the TV Gladiators, the Roman gladiators all had their own styles. Some had swords; some had spears; others had nets. Some gladiators — known as *andabatae* — fought with their eyes covered, which doesn't sound much fun. Most gladiatorial games did have a referee, so hopefully the ancient version of Mark Clattenburg was able to prevent things getting completely out of hand.

Life was hard for the gladiators. Most of them were either slaves, prisoners of war or criminals who had been condemned to fight. They lived in harsh conditions, trained day and night and were lucky to leave with their lives. It's estimated that 8,000 gladiators a year died in combat, and the injured didn't have it much easier. If a fighter was badly hurt, it was often left for the crowd to decide their fate. Worse still, none of the gladiators got to enjoy a post-match interview with Bradley Walsh.

For the lucky few who went unhurt, being a gladiator was like being a rock star. They were rich, famous, and in some cases Roman emperors rewarded their skills by gifting them entire palaces. The best of the best became household names, like Marcus Atticus: a man who actually volunteered to become a gladiator, beat several reigning champions and ended up being commemorated across the city of Pompeii by graffiti artists.

But the gladiators didn't last forever. By the fifth century CE, changing social attitudes and the rise of Christianity caused a steep decline in popularity, and the last ever gladiatorial combat took place in Rome in 404CE. Still, the legacy of the gladiators lives on in artwork, books and film. And on a certain TV show where a guy named after a snake swings on a rope and knocks people off a bridge. Trust us, it's much more fun now.

MAPΓAPEITHC   EΛΛHNIKOC

PUMP-UP PLAYLIST

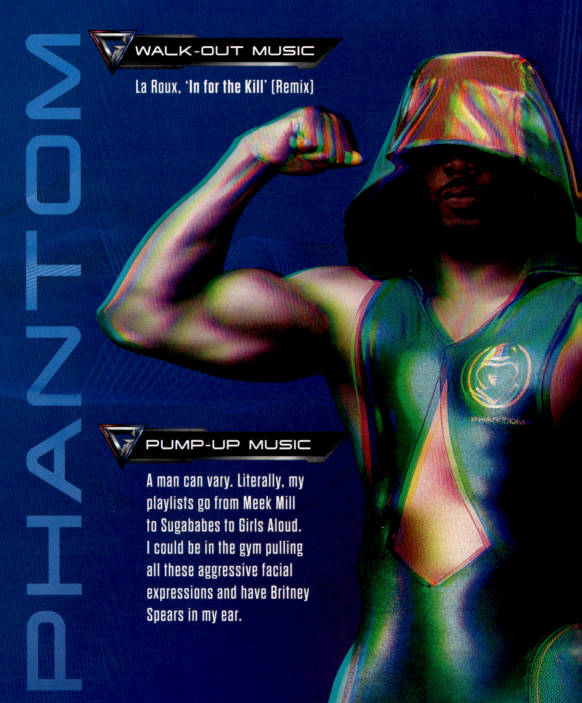

01

PHANTOM

WALK-OUT MUSIC

La Roux, 'In for the Kill' (Remix)

PUMP-UP MUSIC

A man can vary. Literally, my playlists go from Meek Mill to Sugababes to Girls Aloud. I could be in the gym pulling all these aggressive facial expressions and have Britney Spears in my ear.

ATHENA

WALK-OUT MUSIC

Massive Attack,
'Unfinished Sympathy'

PUMP-UP MUSIC

I love Eminem. 'Till I Collapse',
'Lose Yourself', that sort of
thing. This is the sort of music
that really speaks to my soul.

COMET

Dua Lipa ft DaBaby, 'Levitating'

PUMP-UP MUSIC

If I'm strength training, it's either hip hop like Eminem, Drake and Lil Wayne, or rockier stuff like Nickelback. If it's cardio, Hannah Montana [Miley Cyrus] gets played a lot.

BIONIC

 WALK-OUT MUSIC

Chemical Brothers, 'Galvanize'

PUMP-UP MUSIC

Well, I'm not gonna listen to classical music when I'm about to go and bash someone in Duel. Sometimes it's house, sometimes it's rap. Lots of Eminem, always.

VIPER

WALK-OUT MUSIC

Royal Blood, 'Trouble's Coming'

PUMP-UP MUSIC

Viper is rumoured to enjoy listening to 'Snakecharmer' by Rage Against the Machine, 'Snakebite' by Alice Cooper, 'Slither' by Velvet Revolver — and of course anything by Whitesnake. But nobody wants to steal his headphones to find out.

ELECTRO

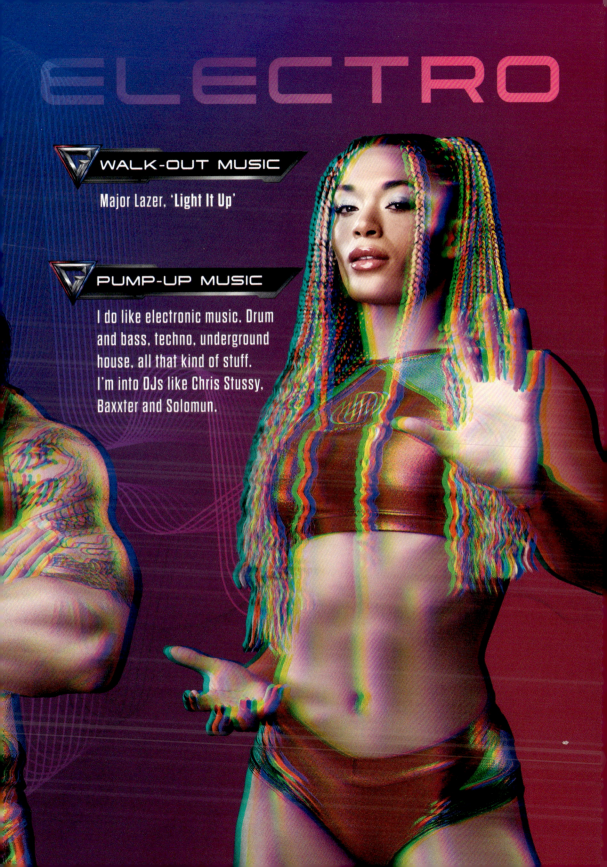

WALK-OUT MUSIC

Major Lazer, 'Light It Up'

PUMP-UP MUSIC

I do like electronic music. Drum and bass, techno, underground house, all that kind of stuff. I'm into DJs like Chris Stussy, Baxxter and Solomun.

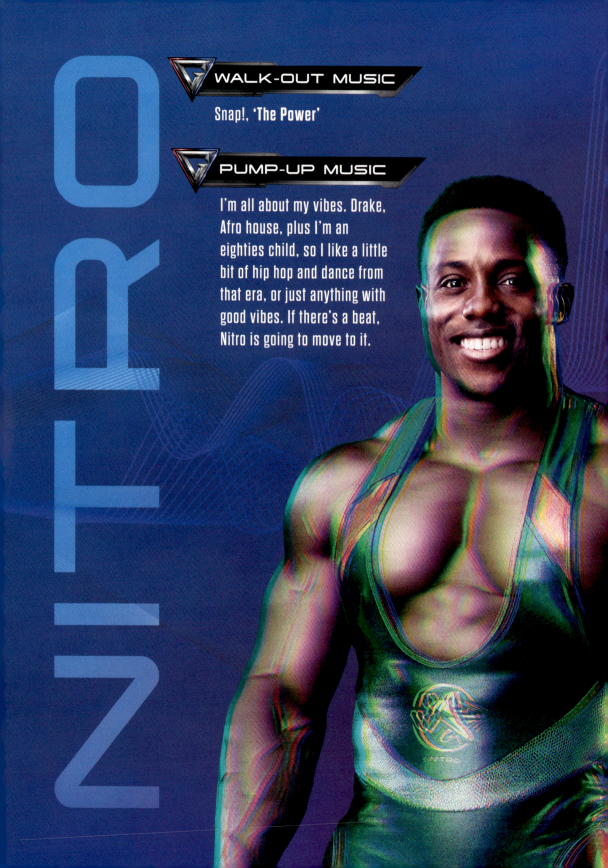

NITRO

WALK-OUT MUSIC

Snap!, 'The Power'

PUMP-UP MUSIC

I'm all about my vibes. Drake, Afro house, plus I'm an eighties child, so I like a little bit of hip hop and dance from that era, or just anything with good vibes. If there's a beat, Nitro is going to move to it.

DIAMOND

WALK-OUT MUSIC

Little Mix ft. Nicki Minaj,
'Woman Like Me'

PUMP-UP MUSIC

Pink is my hype girl for training,
but I'm also a nineties girl, so
I listen to lots of nineties R&B.
And Eminem is always good for
hyping me up, too.

MEET THE GLADIATOR

STATS

HEIGHT: **5 ft 4 in**
BICEP: **36cm**
KEY SKILL: **Strength**

'I love to be surprising. Contenders might think, "I'm taller than her." Yeah — but you're not stronger than me!'

INTRODUCING ATHENA

DID YOU KNOW?

Athena has a small Hang Tough rig set up at home.

MAXIMUM SQUAT

155kg
(heavier than a piano)

MAXIMUM DEADLIFT

185kg
(the same weight as an adult male gorilla)

Athena has never encountered a glass ceiling that she didn't want to smash. The first Sikh woman to represent the UK in powerlifting, she's also the first ever South Asian female Gladiator.

However, she doesn't let herself be defined on those terms. Instead, in the *Gladiators* arena, she is all about getting results. She took part in eight different rounds of Gauntlet in the 2024 series of *Gladiators* alone, and each time she struck fear into the hearts of the contenders who faced her.

As one of the smartest Gladiators, she's all about strategy as well as strength. Underestimate this pocket rocket at your peril.

ABOUT ME

The Athena way

Athena is the goddess of war but also wisdom. I've got the brains and the brawn and I'm here to show you that limits do not exist.

My workout routine

I do weight training about four times a week, I go rock climbing twice a week and I also do wrestling and rugby practice once a week. I train at home at the bottom of the garden.

What I eat

I always joke that the secret to my superpower is my mum's cooking. I tend to have chicken, fish, eggs, the usual. But pasta and rice too. So, healthy eating six days a week, and then on the seventh day I enjoy Indian food like roti, but I'm also not one to shy away from a pizza and ice cream. Basically, I train more so I can eat more.

Growing up

My older brothers went to the same school as me, and they had a reputation as top athletes, so I followed in their footsteps. My PE teacher was pivotal in my journey. When I used to try to set the records on school sports day, he would let me pick which lane I'd want to race in. He would cheekily tell the other students that they were running for second place, which made me very popular as you can imagine!

What I'm like in real life

I'm quite academic – I got a first at university, and a scholarship with a big law firm, plus I'm a qualified accountant. I'm good at strategic thinking, which comes in useful for some of the *Gladiators* events!

My favourite event on *Gladiators* …

My favourite events are the strength-related ones. I do love Powerball, especially when you get to tackle and run after contenders.

… and my least favourite

Not that I dislike Duel, but you're quite high up in the air, and those platforms wobble! So you have to combat the fear and natural instinct of not wanting to fall off as well as fight. You might just lose your balance and fall … which I may or may not have done!

My journey

I'm the first Sikh woman to represent Great Britain at the World and European Championships. Being a South Asian woman in strength sports, I'm pretty much a unicorn. Traditionally, this isn't something that we're supposed to do – there's an expectation that you should focus on education. So I studied hard, but I also wanted to show everyone that there's more to life. If you're disciplined and dedicated, you can be good at other things too. I really get a kick out of breaking that stereotype and I'm a huge advocate for women's sport. I want to blaze a trail.

My hero

My dad is a former bodybuilder and powerlifter, and he's trained me since I was a little girl. He always showed us that hard work and determination can get you anywhere in life. Also, my mum comes from a family of wrestling champions. After she had kids, she went out and won five golds and four silver medals at track and field events. She's all about breaking barriers. But I think it's important to be your own role model, too.

What I've learned

When I fell off the podium during a round of Duel, it was horrible. I didn't want to watch it back. But I learned that at the end of the day, you just have to laugh it

GET THE LOOK

I always have braids in my hair and very striking gold eyeshadow. I wear a crop top and shorts, because it's all about looking good, but also being functional. I have Wonder Woman-style cuffs, because I wear a kara – a Sikh bangle – that I need to cover for safety. But my favourite thing is my emblem, an owl. My dream has always been to help women who are denied opportunity in sports, to give them their wings to fly. So I'm happy my emblem has wings.

off. You can't change what happened, because you're in front of 3,000 people. Sometimes in life you have to fall flat on your face to get better at getting back up. If the Gladiators were winning all the time, it wouldn't be entertaining.

BE CHALLENGE-READY

So, you think you have what it takes to beat the Gladiators?

As well as being the show's Assistant Referee, Lee Phillips is also so fit that he could pass as a Gladiator himself. In fact, he is the guy who designed the show's fitness tests. When the Gladiators and contenders were auditioning, he was the man who put them through their paces.

This means that he is the best person to help you get into shape for each *Gladiators* event. If you're planning on taking down the Gladiators any time soon, here are the drills he suggests.

Hang Tough

If you've ever seen the video of Sabre yanking her full weight down on a contender as they cling onto the rings, you'll know that colossal grip strength will get you further than anything here. 'Pull-ups will really help you here,' says Lee. 'And one way to improve your grip strength is by doing a dead hang off a pull-up bar. Just jump up, grab the bar and see how long you can hang there. Start off by doing four sets of thirty-second hangs with a minute break in between, and then the following week go for forty-five seconds. The event is only a minute long, but don't forget that for some of that time a Gladiator might be wrapped around you, trying to pull you down. Grip strength is everything here.'

The Wall

The only real way to train to launch yourself up a giant climbing wall at top speed is, well, to launch yourself up a giant climbing wall at top speed. However, if you don't have a giant climbing wall to hand, Lee has some alternative ideas. 'The Wall is all about pulling strength, so again I'd recommend pull-ups on an overhead bar,' he says. 'Don't worry if you can't do a full bodyweight pull-up yet, because you can buy resistance bands that will help take some of the weight off at first until you build up your strength.

'The thing they don't tell you about Duel is that the platforms wobble a lot when you're up there,'
LEE

You also need good mobility, so something like yoga will help a lot with that. And don't forget, The Wall is tall. If you're not good with heights now, get used to them.'

Duel

Don't be fooled. Duel might look like an event that you need enormous arms for, but the real strength you need comes from somewhere else. 'The thing they don't tell you about Duel is that the platforms wobble a lot when you're up there,' says Lee. 'This means you need to strengthen your core, ideally on some sort of unstable platform. Maybe try balancing on a half exercise ball for as long as you can, or even do some weighted exercises on one. A strong core is a must for this one, because otherwise, well ... if Giant wallops you up there, he's going to knock you straight off.'

Powerball

There is a certain breed of Gladiator – like Fury and Apollo – who are experts at contact sports like rugby. They love Powerball because it gives them an excuse to smash into you as hard as they can. If you're a contender, the best way to train for this is to learn how to avoid getting tackled. 'This one is all about agility, and there are plenty of running drills you can do,' says Lee. 'Set up a series of cones and practise running around them. This will teach you to quickly change direction at speed, which is what you need if you don't want to get clobbered.'

Gauntlet

The Gladiators might find Gauntlet challenging, but it's a much harder event

for contenders, requiring them to pick up speed over and over again, from a standing start, to clatter past their opponents.

'In Gauntlet, you're facing these huge Gladiators, so you'll just need sheer power for this one,' Lee says. 'So strength training is the only thing for it. Try to build up lots of strength in your legs, and gain as much explosive power as you can, because the event doesn't give you much of a run-up. Explosive exercises like jumps while holding weights will be brilliant for this, and will really help you barge through the Glads.'

Collision

If you're a Gladiator, this might be the easiest event of all. All they need to do is swing on a rope and try to knock the contenders off the bridge. But as a contender, it's much more difficult to navigate the maze of high-speed Gladiator thighs coming at you. 'You're basically running on an unstable structure here, so balance and coordination are key,' says Lee. 'This means more core training. But also, don't forget that you're allowed to push the Gladiators away as they swing at you, and for that you'll need really good upper body strength.'

The Edge

Everyone is intimidated by The Edge, both contenders and Gladiators, so much so that Fury has even set up a special piece of equipment at home to help her train for it. You don't need to go to those extremes, however. 'Like Powerball, this one is all about speed and the ability to change direction in the blink of an eye,' says Lee. 'But the main thing you need here is confidence. Even though there's a net underneath you, you're still really high. It's a shock to a lot of contenders the first time they do it for real, and having a good head for heights is the only way to counter that.'

The Ring

'Just like Powerball, this is another contact event, but with one crucial difference. The Ring is all about speed and agility to get around the Gladiators as quickly as possible to get to the central ring itself,' says Lee. But because the button is low down, you have to be good at throwing yourself down on the ground and getting back up quickly. Lee says, 'There's no better training for this than a burpee. In fact, we use burpees quite a lot when we're testing the fitness of our contenders. They're really good, and they're bodyweight exercises so you don't need any equipment either.'

'It's a shock to a lot of contenders the first time they do it for real, and having a good head for heights is the only way to counter that.'
LEE

The Eliminator

Now it's time for the big finale.

'This is a properly tricky one, because there's so much involved in it,' says Lee. 'The first thing, maybe even the most important thing, is to learn how to climb a rope. If you can't do that efficiently you're going to tire yourself out really quickly and lose a lot of time getting up it. Then there's the overhead ladder, which is all about grip strength and upper body, and then even more upper body when you get to the cargo net and zipwire.

'One big potential stumbling block is the balance beam. You might think it looks quite easy, but remember that when the contenders are doing that they are fatigued and if they fall off they lose crucial seconds. So set a balance beam up at home, or even just draw a line on the floor, then get your heart rate up on some cardio equipment and have a go. I guarantee that you'll find balancing a lot harder when you're tired.

'And then it's the big one. The Travelator is all about pure leg speed, so you'll need to do lots of sprints. Set a treadmill to a steep incline and then do interval sprints on it, so you get used to running flat out uphill from a standing start. There are lots of different elements.'

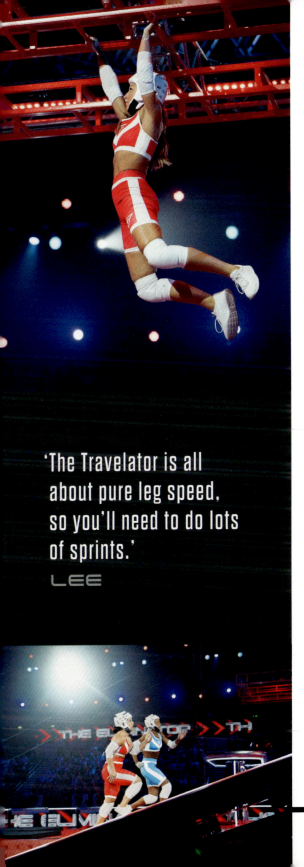

'If you want to have any chance beating the Gladiators, you're going to need every skill at your disposal.'

'The Travelator is all about pure leg speed, so you'll need to do lots of sprints.'

LEE

In summary

Anything that raises your basic level of fitness is a good thing. But Lee points out that the most important thing is to 'have a broad range of skills', whether it's running, weightlifting or gymnastics. Aim for what's known as functional fitness – strength training that readies your body for real-life activities. We're talking pushing, pulling, bending, twisting, lifting, loading, squatting and core work. If you want to have any chance of beating the Gladiators, it's no use concentrating on just one thing – you're going to need every skill at your disposal.

MEET THE GLADIATOR

STATS

HEIGHT: **5 ft 10 in**
WINGSPAN: **188cm**
KEY SKILL: **Speed**

'You can have fun near the flames,
but come too close and you'll get burnt.'

INTRODUCING FIRE

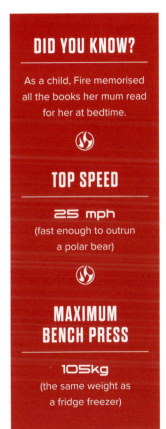

DID YOU KNOW?

As a child, Fire memorised all the books her mum read for her at bedtime.

TOP SPEED

25 mph
(fast enough to outrun a polar bear)

MAXIMUM BENCH PRESS

105kg
(the same weight as a fridge freezer)

So far on *Gladiators*, Fire has proved herself to be remarkably versatile. Like Phantom, she comes from a background of sprinting and bobsledding, and she uses this explosive power to her advantage. She's taken out more contenders than any other female Gladiator on Collision and is so far undefeated in Duel.

These breathtaking achievements come from having the mind of an athlete. Fire chases victory, and achieves it more than most, but she also knows how to shake off defeat with a smile, learn from her mistakes and come back better than ever.

Never underestimate the danger of Fire – you'd be making a big mistake if you do.

ABOUT ME

The Fire way

I'm lots of fun, very playful, but still hugely competitive. People always want to play with fire but be careful, it can be a bit fierce.

My workout routine

I work out three hours a day, four days a week. I sprint and I lift. Those are the two main components that I do. Lots of sprinting, lots of lifting.

What I eat

My approach to eating is very relaxed. I don't calorie count or anything like that. My diet is much more performance-based rather than about trying to achieve a certain look. I try to eat clean – four meals a day, no fast food. Lots of protein, but always quite balanced. The only thing I really have as a treat is popcorn. I'm a popcorn fiend.

Growing up

I was highly academic at school. All top sets. I did chat a lot, obviously, but I was always top of my class, a prefect, honours, all that jazz. And I'm still studying. I've got three degrees and I'm on the road to a PhD, if I ever get round to finishing it.

What I'm like in real life

I've competed in both the summer and winter Olympics and not many people can say that! Summer came first, because I was a sprinter for fifteen years. But then I repeatedly got asked to join the bobsleigh team. So I gave it a go, did the trials and broke the testing record. You have to be made of tough stuff to bobsleigh; it's very powerful and fast at the same time, plus you have to be fearless. It's an adrenaline sport; Formula One on ice. It can be really dangerous if you get it wrong. Some people just freeze up and can't do it. But those who can, bobsleigh!

My favourite event on *Gladiators* ...

Powerball. It's just a muscle tussle. It's a team game, plus you get to take people down. I love all that.

... and my least favourite

I don't like The Edge because it's very high up. I'm not great with heights, so I'm dealing with my fear at the same time as trying to take someone down.

My journey

I've had a couple of major injuries in my life. One of them was so bad it needed knee surgery. When it happened, the doctors said, 'Your career is probably done.' I couldn't walk for three months. It wasn't just the physical issues that I had to deal with, but also the mental anguish, knowing that I might not be able to come back from it. I'd gone from being the fastest British woman of all time to someone who couldn't even walk to the bathroom on her own. But I did come back, and I won a medal at the Commonwealth Games within ten months. It meant so much, and it wasn't about the medal. It was about resilience.

My hero

My mum has been such a strong woman. To have raised me and my brother to be decent individuals in this world is a testament to her kind nature. She always makes people feel like their own Gladiator. Also, my old training partner, Donna Fraser, is a big inspiration to me. She's a four-time British Olympian and cancer survivor. She's an advocate for diversity and inclusivity, and for moving on from difficulties and never giving up. She taught me how to be an athlete when I was sixteen.

What I've learned

Gladiators has taught me that, no matter who you're facing, ultimately you're always going up against yourself. It's

GET THE LOOK

The most important thing is to always keep a smile on your face. There's also the move, where you blow the contenders away with a fireball, but you've got to remember to give them the eyes. Do it with a cheeky smile.

how you approach a challenge and your integrity throughout the challenge that counts. I've learned that being the best version of myself, for everyone else around me, is the most important thing to me. It doesn't matter if you win or lose, it's how you do it that's important.

BUMPS & BRUISES

As fun as it is to watch, it's important to remember that *Gladiators* is a show that requires full-blast physical effort from everyone involved. As such, it's no surprise that sometimes people get hurt. Two of the Gladiators in the 2024 series suffered injuries during events, which put their futures in jeopardy. Thanks to expert treatment and iron-clad determination, they will both make it back for the 2025 series. Here are their stories.

Comet

During a round of Hang Tough, Comet fell from the rings awkwardly and broke her ankle. At the time, she says that her first priority was to keep smiling and finish the event. 'I have a very high pain threshold and too much pride to let the audience know that I was hurt,' she remembers. As such, since she couldn't walk, she decided to forward-roll off the mat to keep the pressure off her foot. 'I still did the post-event interview, and you wouldn't know anything was wrong,' she says. 'I think it was pure adrenaline, plus I had a job to do.'

Backstage, she started to realise that something was badly wrong. 'I got assessed and then taken for scans, and that's when I found out how bad it was,' Comet says. Her ankle was not only fractured twice, but dislocated. She underwent surgery, and now has two metal plates in her ankle. Recovery took time. 'I was out for a good seven or eight

'I have a very high pain threshold and too much pride to let the audience know that I was hurt.'

COMET

months,' she says. 'I had to lie on my back for two weeks straight. I could not move. It wasn't until five or six months after it happened that I started learning to walk again. But I did everything I could to make sure I had the speediest recovery possible. I did rehab and physio, plus I trained my upper body and swam whenever I could. It was hard, but now I'm back and ready for the next series!'

Sabre

Meanwhile, Sabre made it to the semi-finals before suffering an injury. It happened during The Edge, and it was only once she was down that she discovered that her hamstring had been torn from her bone. 'I'm back to 100 per cent now,' she says. 'I'm training in full again, but it's been a long road back. The injury prevented me from doing anything. I couldn't walk for a month.'

But, like Comet, she made a remarkable recovery. Sabre's schedule required four rehab sessions for the first two months after the injury, along with multiple physiotherapy sessions and massages. She credits her coach, her friends and her fellow Gladiators for giving her the support necessary to bounce back as quickly as she did. 'And now I'm back to the athlete I know I am,' she says.

The backstage team

Holding things together when things go wrong is a team of paramedics, doctors and sports therapists.

Alfie Martin, one of the show's sports rehabilitators, along with his team Sarah and Kirsty, take care of everyone's physical niggles during filming, and administer physiotherapy whenever things take a turn for the worse.

'If any of the Gladiators wanted a consultation, they could roll in between nine and eleven in the morning, write their names on a whiteboard and we'd just work our way through them,' he says.

It was a good thing they were there: almost everyone who appeared on *Gladiators* sustained some sort of injury over the course of the 2024 series, and we're not just talking about the contenders. Bionic hurt his ankle, Legend broke a finger and Fury dislocated a thumb. 'We had a quad tear, a rotator cuff injury and some ACL injuries, too,' Alfie says. 'We also had a lot of skin issues from being on the ropes, and a few rolled ankles. Surprisingly, we also had to deal with a lot of forearm tendonitis: the Gladiators are so big and heavy that when they're swinging or climbing, their forearms are just working overtime.'

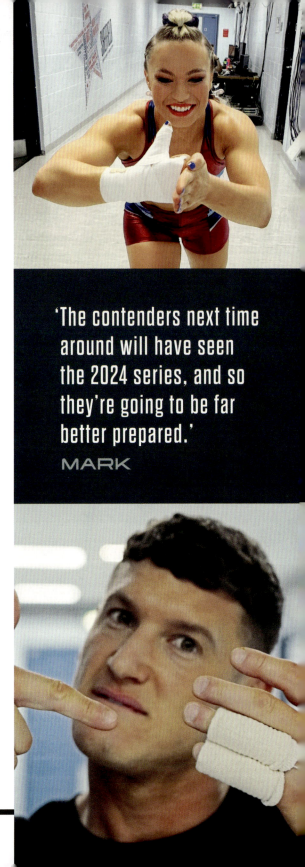

'The contenders next time around will have seen the 2024 series, and so they're going to be far better prepared.'
MARK

And don't think that these injuries will be a one-off, either. 'The 2025 series is going to be dynamite,' promises Referee Mark Clattenburg. 'The contenders next time around will have seen the 2024 series, and so they're going to be far better prepared. It's going to be much more of a challenge for the Gladiators to stop them, and they're really going to be ready to give the Gladiators what for.'

This means that the potential for injury could be even higher next time around. Especially since, as Clattenburg reveals, the Gladiators have anticipated the challenge.

'I saw some of them recently,' he says. 'They've been training harder too. They know what's going to face them, and so many of them are so much bigger than they were in *Gladiators* 2024. They're stronger, because they all want to be the best. The contenders will need to be at the top of their game if they want to score any points.'

MEET THE GLADIATOR

STATS

HEIGHT: **5 ft 11 in**
STRIDE LENGTH: **2.35m**
BICEP: **44cm**

'I'm always running, jumping, dancing.
There's no catching me;
I have that Nitro energy in me!'

NITRO

INTRODUCING NITRO

DID YOU KNOW?

Nitro likes to ambush the other Gladiators with brainteasers. Steel enjoys them a lot, but Sabre runs away.

TOP SPEED

27 mph

(as fast as a car on most urban roads)

LONGEST STANDING JUMP

3.65m

(longer than three adult sheep in a line)

Nitro is known for his ability to radiate positivity at every turn.

In events, this attitude means he's always the first to congratulate contenders, regardless of whether they've won or lost. But behind the scenes he's just as sunny. If you ever see the Gladiators in a huddle, it's probably because he initiated it. If you ever hear them singing karaoke, it's probably because he has encouraged them to join in.

This is either a sign that his cheeky winning smile is truly infectious, or that there's no point trying to avoid him because he's so much faster than everybody else.

ABOUT ME

The Nitro way

The Nitro way is pure PMA – positive mental attitude – along with an explosive sense of force, hitting you right in the face. Plus I'm an amazing dancer.

My workout routine

I'm a sprinter, so I'm on the track four days a week, focusing on accelerations and high-speed running. And then I'm in the gym, mainly doing a bit of conditioning. I also do a bit of climbing too, and some gymnastics so my body can move a bit more freely.

What I eat

A lot of protein, but I'm all about the good vibes, so I treat myself too. So as much as I train hard, and eat very clean, I also love to cook. My mum always taught me that if you like something, learn how to make it, so I've just learned how to make my own pizzas. And then at the end of the day I'll bake a cake or a chocolate fondant or a brownie. Whatever I fancy.

Growing up

School was all good vibes for me. I could hang out with anyone – I had lots of sporty friends and I have a geek side too, so I also had pals in chess club. But it just so happens that the gods also gave me all the skills I needed to be able to run up and down a football pitch and score lots of goals. I became the fastest youth runner in the world of all time when I was fourteen, and then won BBC Young Sports Personality of the Year at sixteen, and that's when sport took over my life.

What I'm like in real life

I like to be in the moment, all the time. So if a fan comes up and asks me for anything, like my signature or some advice, I will never deny them, especially if it's a kid. You never know what those children are going to grow up to become.

My favourite event on *Gladiators* ...

Duel. Some of the Gladiators like to get the contenders off as quickly as possible, but I like to milk it. I don't want to knock them down in one. I'm always trying to think how to make my moves look cool. My goal is to play with the contenders a bit and then have some fun. I imagine I'm playing a computer game: boom, boom, WHACK, jump up and spin around.

... and my least favourite

Me and The Edge need to have a conversation! It's difficult trying to express the power that I have when I'm on it. I've got to really spend a bit of time on that piece of equipment to figure out how it can handle my power.

My journey

I feel like I was born to be a Gladiator. As an athlete, I've had twenty years of preparation for this job. I am quite lucky that my talent and mindset have enabled me to be a strong all-rounder when it comes to the events. I've worked hard for everything I do, so I'm learning how to embrace my specialness. It isn't very British of me in that respect. If we were American, we'd be comfortable talking about how amazing we are, but us Brits, we love to make a joke to bring ourselves down a peg or two.

My hero

I literally dressed up as Superman all the time when I was a kid. I loved Superman. Then once I got into my teenage years, I started seeing all these real people like Linford Christie and David Beckham who taught me that even if you can't win, it doesn't mean that you shouldn't try your hardest. And then there's Usain Bolt. Incredible. I got to run with him right at the moment when he was becoming an icon, which was amazing to witness.

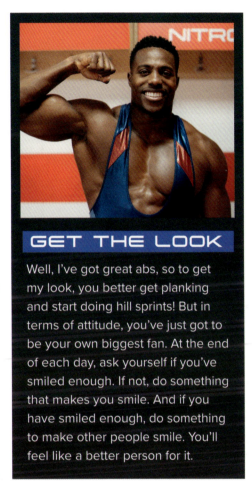

GET THE LOOK

Well, I've got great abs, so to get my look, you better get planking and start doing hill sprints! But in terms of attitude, you've just got to be your own biggest fan. At the end of each day, ask yourself if you've smiled enough. If not, do something that makes you smile. And if you have smiled enough, do something to make other people smile. You'll feel like a better person for it.

What I've learned

Being on *Gladiators* has taught me not to question my ability. We are superheroes and the arena is our HQ. I've learned how much I appreciate the rest of the team as well, having the others to bounce off. I never had that before, doing an individual sport, but here we all come together and it's great.

THE EDGE

HOW IT WORKS

One of the newest events, The Edge is just as challenging for the Gladiators as it is for contenders. Taking place nine metres above the arena floor – the height of two double-decker buses – The Edge is a daunting network of narrow beams that must be crossed without falling, or without being tackled off the structure by a Gladiator. Get your strategy right and contenders can make a fool of the Gladiator. Hesitate for even a second, though, and it's a long way down. The fall is no joke, either: this is the event that tore Sabre's hamstring in *Gladiators* 2024.

BASICS

TIME LIMIT: **60** secs
GLADIATORS: **1**
CONTENDERS: **1**
WEAPONS: **None**

SCORING

FOR EACH SUCCESSFUL CROSS
(HEATS & QUARTER-FINALS): **3** POINTS
(SEMIS & FINAL): **2** POINTS

> 'Hesitate for even a second, and it's a long way down.'

(for the 2024 series)

The contender must attempt to cross to score points, which are capped at 18 points in the heats and quarter-finals and 15 points in the semis and finals.

———

The Gladiator may prevent the contenders from crossing by blocking them, tackling them or simply forcing them off the playing surface into the net below.

———

If a contender accidentally falls off, the event is over. If a Gladiator falls off, the contender may continue to cross.

SKILLS

SPEED: ▽ ▽ ▽ ▽ ▽

STRENGTH: ▽ ▽ ▽ ▽ ▽

AGILITY: ▽ ▽ ▽ ▽ ▽

BRAVERY: ▽ ▽ ▽ ▽ ▽

THE RING

HOW IT WORKS

Another new event, The Ring is a floor-based contact game where contenders must hit a button in the middle of the playing area to score. As always, though, they find themselves facing a Gladiator who is tasked with taking them down as brutally as possible. The Ring is the ultimate test of strength and agility, so contenders need to operate at speed here – either to dodge their opposing Gladiator or (if they enjoy living dangerously) crash into them on purpose.

BASICS

TIME LIMIT: **60** secs
GLADIATORS: **2**
CONTENDERS: **2**
WEAPONS: **None**

SCORING

EACH TIME THE BUTTON IS HIT: **2** POINTS

'The Ring is the ultimate test of strength and agility.'

RULES

The contenders score points by hitting the central button, protected by two Gladiators.

———

Contenders can score by hitting the button with any part of their body.

———

No punching, kicking, body-slamming or elbowing.

SKILLS

SPEED: ▽ ▽ ▽ ▽ ▽

STRENGTH: ▽ ▽ ▽ ▽ ▽

AGILITY: ▽ ▽ ▽ ▽ ▽

BRAVERY: ▽ ▽ ▽ ▽ ▽

GLADIATORS

COLLISION

HOW IT WORKS

For the Gladiators, Collision almost counts as a day off. All they have to do is swing backwards and forwards on a trapeze and hope they make contact. But for the contenders, this is one of the toughest tests to face. To score, they have to carry a ball across a precarious thirteen-metre suspension bridge, hung three metres in the air, with nothing to grab on to – then throw it into a goal at the other side. What's more, four hulking great trapezing Gladiators are making it their mission to boot the contenders off the bridge. One wrong move and they get a Gladiator's thigh in their face and it's all over. This is an epic test of timing as well as speed.

BASICS

TIME LIMIT: **60** secs
GLADIATORS: **4**
CONTENDERS: **1**
WEAPONS: **None**

SCORING

FOR EVERY BALL IN THE NET: **2** POINTS

'One wrong move and they get a Gladiator's thigh in their face and it's all over.'

COMPETE LIKE A GLADIATOR

As physically impressive as the Gladiators are, perhaps the most impressive thing about them is their sense of sportsmanship. Win or lose, they'll (almost) always be up on their feet congratulating the contender the second the final whistle blows. If you want some tips on how to compete with dignity, you've come to the right place.

Play hard, but don't hold grudges

Nobody typifies this mindset quite like Fury. A former rugby player, she takes no prisoners on the pitch. 'Your opponent isn't your friend,' she says. 'You're rivals, so you crack on. But whatever happens,

when the match ends, you go and shake their hand. Even if you've just lost and it's heart-wrenching, you support each other. Because you're all there for the same reason. We all love sport.'

Respect your opponent

If you've watched enough *Gladiators*, you'll know that Nitro has one of the healthiest attitudes when an event ends. 'Anytime I go up against someone, I always use the post-event interview to tell the world how good my opponent was,' he says. And these are no empty compliments, either. 'Just the very fact that a contender is facing us is honourable. We're Gladiators, so they're already at a disadvantage, and the chances are they were always going to lose. Just the

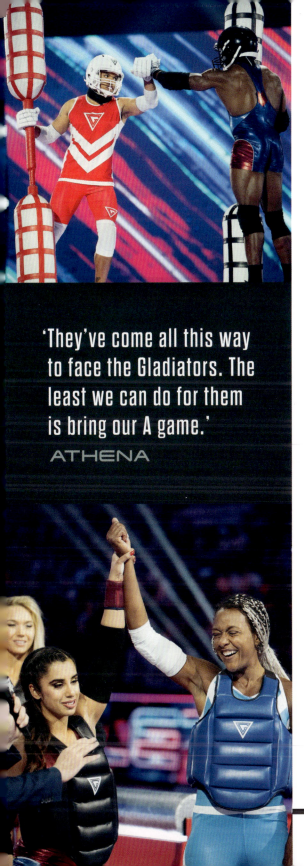

'They've come all this way to face the Gladiators. The least we can do for them is bring our A game.'

ATHENA

fact that they were brave enough to step up is something that should be applauded and respected.'

Give your all

Part of being a Gladiator, Diamond says, is giving the contender what they came for. Put simply, that's the fight of their lives. Going easy on them would be unfair on them; that's not what they are here for. 'In the heat of the moment it's super important to compose yourself, but not so much that you pull back on that competitiveness. We have to find the right balance between being respectful, but also letting the contenders know that they're not in for an easy ride. We're always going to give you everything we've got.'

'They've come all this way to face the Gladiators,' adds Athena. 'The least we can do for them is bring our A game.'

If you lose, lose with grace ...

The short lesson here is to do the opposite of whatever Viper does when he loses. Don't sulk. Don't snarl. Definitely don't grab Bradley Walsh's microphone and try to bite it in half.

Instead, you'd be wise to take a leaf out of Fire's attitude to losing. 'There's a real skill when it comes to learning how to lose with grace,' she says. 'You really have to know yourself. A big part of it is congratulating the winner. I'll always say "well done" if someone does well, because I know how hard it is to put yourself out there.'

... and then learn from it

This is the scariest part of talking to a Gladiator. As much as they'll shake your hand if you beat them, they will also decide never to let it happen again. 'I have the mindset of "you never truly lose, you only learn",' says Apollo. 'There are no losses, there are only lessons. Losing is a part of life, and those who can deal with it the best are the ones who will continue to evolve.'

Or, as Electro puts it, 'We're competitive people. If you beat me, that's cool, I'll take it on the chin. But you should know that I'm going to come back even better. I'm just gonna hit twice as hard next time.'

Sabre has a similar philosophy. 'My mum always instilled in me that you have to thank the bull that bucked you off, because they're the ones that encourage you to get better,' she says. 'So when I lose, I commend the person who beat me. But then I remember why they beat me, and practise that. I do it every time.'

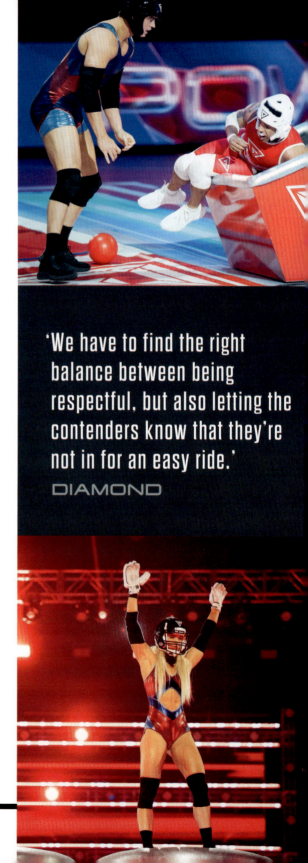

'We have to find the right balance between being respectful, but also letting the contenders know that they're not in for an easy ride.'
DIAMOND

Remember, nobody's perfect

Then again, everyone slips up from time to time. During a particularly tense round of Gauntlet in the 2024 series, Sabre threw off her pads and angrily charged at a contender for the crime of trash-talking her. The same event ended with Diamond getting in the Referee's face for siding with a contender in a dispute. 'I hate losing,' Diamond says. 'I just really hate losing. You'll see it in my face when I lose, I'll just get really stroppy.' You sense that she still hasn't got over her Gauntlet blowout either, in that whenever anyone brings it up, she seethes, 'Oh, now you've really got my back up.'

So they can do their best to be magnanimous – but even the Gladiators have a human side every once in a while. With the possible exception of Viper, of course!

You are your only real competitor

Fire knows that her only real battle is with herself. 'The real fight is always against yourself,' she says. 'Even if you're the best at something, there will always come a time when someone is better than you. So you have to focus on yourself, and bring your A game, no matter what. It's important to always have integrity in what you do. It's a personal thing to me. But I think everyone has that inner strength, to some extent.'

So always set an example

'We're role models,' Athena points out. 'There are kids in the crowd and watching at home, and it doesn't look good if we kick off every time we lose an event. We want to win, of course we do, but we also want the contenders to enjoy their experience with us. So, win or lose, it's really important to demonstrate some sportsmanship. You never know who's watching the show so that means we always have to carry ourselves with a certain amount of grace.'

Alternatively, just be like Legend

'I don't know how to lose with dignity, because I don't lose,' says Legend unhelpfully.

Honestly, some people are just a lost cause.

MEET THE GLADIATOR

STATS

HEIGHT: **6 ft**
BICEP: **36cm**
QUADS: **60cm**

'Diamonds are unbreakable.'

INTRODUCING DIAMOND

DID YOU KNOW?

Diamond will often perform a one-minute happy dance when she is served food, because food makes her joyful. But don't steal from her plate. 'I'm like Joey from *Friends*. I don't share.' Also, her favourite breakfast when she was a child was toast dipped in porridge.

MAXIMUM HIP THRUST

220kg
(heavier than two adult seals)

MAXIMUM SQUAT

160kg
(the same weight as seventy bricks)

Towering over the other female Gladiators, the statuesque and mighty Diamond always stands out in a crowd. But behind her glamorous image, you'll find one of the most competitive Gladiators on the show.

Diamond always wants to win, no matter what. But although this drive can sometimes take over – the other Gladiators are all in agreement that she's the worst loser out of the female Gladiators – Diamond is always quick to regain her composure and move on to the next challenge.

She isn't someone you'd want as an enemy, but Diamond is a good friend and a brilliant competitor.

ABOUT ME

The Diamond way

I want to empower everyone to be the best they can be, and to embrace their unique selves.

My workout routine

I love training! I go to the gym twice a day, six times a week. I do a split of bodybuilding and functional training. With bodybuilding, I'll train my chest, shoulders and triceps one day, then my back and biceps another day. I do two leg days, split between quads and glutes and hamstrings and glutes. And then around that, I go to a gymnastics class, because that really helps everything that you need to be a Gladiator.

What I eat

I stick to a daily calorie intake, and a daily protein goal, because protein is important to help you build muscle. So I eat lots of chicken, and I also make my own sushi.

Growing up

I was a tomboy and really into my sport. I was the girl who constantly had her hair tied up playing football with the boys. As soon as I got into the playground, I was playing football straight away, just super competitive. I wouldn't say I was an A-class student, but I tried my hardest. Unfortunately, I was bullied all through school for being tall and different, and wanting to play sport with the boys. But now I realise that all the things I was bullied for gave me my superpower.

What I'm like in real life

I'm extremely competitive. I always give everything 100 per cent. At school I played football, cricket, rounders, high jump, and I swam at county level. It made me versatile, and it gave me a team mentality, which has been really useful on *Gladiators*. But I do hate losing. I'm a real sore loser. I don't hold a grudge, but I can get very stroppy.

My favourite event on *Gladiators* ...

Honestly, I love all of them. The most intense is Duel. There's a lot of pressure, being one-to-one with the contenders. But I use the Diamond stare on the contenders before we start, which is very piercing, and I always get the first hit in. I don't give them a chance!

... and my least favourite

Even though I enjoy The Wall, it was sometimes really annoying because the contenders' shoes kept coming off in my hands. That really got under my skin, and I complained to the Referees about it. I ended up throwing one of the shoes across the arena, because it didn't seem fair.

My journey

Like I said, I was bullied quite badly all through school. Sport helped with that, because it was my escape. Being bullied was horrible, but it helped me to become the strong person I am today. That's why I want to show young girls or boys that you can still be your unique self, even when you're getting bullied. You don't have to change who you are. You should embrace it, because who knows where that's going to take you?

My hero

I grew up idolising the old Gladiators from the 1990s. But as far as my sports are concerned, I couldn't have done it without the encouragement from my family. The day I came home from school and said I wanted to play football, my dad was like, 'OK! Let's find you a football team to play on!' No questions or worries, just total support. Having that support behind me helped me become the person I am today.

What I've learned

Being on *Gladiators* has taught me to be prepared for anything and everything. You never know what a contender is going to do – whether it's shaking a shoe off on The Wall, or trying to dodge us on The Ring. I'm not afraid when I'm hit on the head on Duel. Some of the contenders give it back as good as they get, and fair play to them.

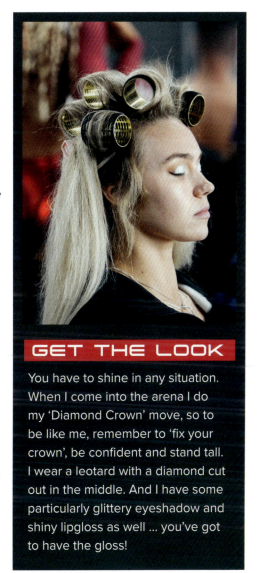

GET THE LOOK

You have to shine in any situation. When I come into the arena I do my 'Diamond Crown' move, so to be like me, remember to 'fix your crown', be confident and stand tall. I wear a leotard with a diamond cut out in the middle. And I have some particularly glittery eyeshadow and shiny lipgloss as well ... you've got to have the gloss!

MEET THE REFEREES

Gladiators is a show full of extremely impressive people, from the shiny, beefed-up Gladiators themselves to the contenders brave enough to try and take them on. But secretly, the most impressive people of all might be the show's Referees. They need the intelligence to know all the rules inside out, and the authority to enforce them and make sure nobody cheats. They also need big enough personalities to stand up to the Gladiators whenever they cross the line.

Luckily, *Gladiators* boasts some of the best Referees around. Mark Clattenburg, along with his Assistants Sonia Mkoloma and Lee Phillips, are all titans in their field. Mark has refereed football matches to the highest level, Sonia has won medals at the Commonwealth Games, and Lee once held the title of 'Ultimate Firefighter'. Together, they are the people who keep the whole show on the road. Let's find out a little bit more about them.

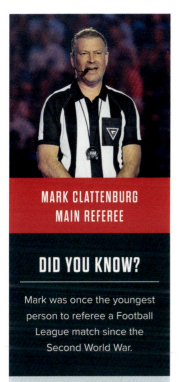

**MARK CLATTENBURG
MAIN REFEREE**

DID YOU KNOW?

Mark was once the youngest person to referee a Football League match since the Second World War.

'I get tweets all the time from people who think I'm putting on a Scottish accent when I shout "Gladiators, ready!" I'm really not. That's just how I sound!'

MARK

Mark is a former professional football referee, who oversaw the 2012 Men's Olympics final, the 2014 European Super Cup, the 2016 FA Cup, the 2016 Champions League final and the 2016 European Championships final.

How I got the job
John Anderson, the Referee from the 1990s series, was absolutely iconic. But for the 2024 series, the producers decided to go with a new refereeing team. I got the call to do some role plays to demonstrate what I could bring to the show. When I got the job, it was a real 'pinch me' moment! John's a hard act to follow, but I'm so happy to be here.

Challenges of the job
Gladiators is a fun TV show, but the rules need to be followed. It's a difficult balance to get right, because it isn't entertaining if I keep coming in and stopping an event, but it's also important that everything is as it should be. There's still a huge sporting element that needs to be overseen. Everyone taking part is competitive.

Toughest event
The Edge doesn't look that scary on TV, but when you're up there and it's rocking, it's terrifying. I'm not very good at heights, so sometimes I'm shaking with fear up there.

Sneakiest Gladiator to referee
Legend is a fantastic athlete, but he likes to wind me up on The Edge. He knows I'm scared of heights, so he'll deliberately jump up and down on it to make it rock. Sometimes when I see Legend messing about, I want the contender to win, just to shut him up.

SONIA

Sonia is a former England netball player, who competed in five Netball World Cups and three Commonwealth Games before becoming Assistant Coach to the England netball team. She is now the Head Coach of the second team and the England Roses Academy. She's also a trained social worker.

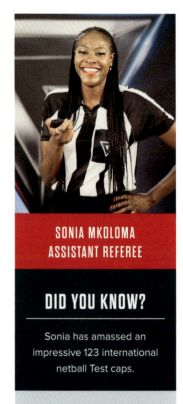

**SONIA MKOLOMA
ASSISTANT REFEREE**

How I got the job
The producers slid into my DMs! Last year, I got an Instagram message saying, 'Hey, we're from *Gladiators*, would you be interested in trying out to be a Referee in the new series?' I thought it was a joke, but I replied and it all just snowballed from there. Someone at *Gladiators* must be a netball fan!

Challenges of the job
I'm from a sporting background, so I know that there will always be people who will try to bend the rules. You just have to keep your wits about you and stay in charge.

Toughest event
There was so much controversy about The Wall! Contenders will always do whatever it takes to win, and sometimes that means loose shoes. As refs, we have to try to check their laces to make sure they're tight enough. But we'll also remind the Gladiators that if you grab someone's shoe, it'll probably come off. Like, you're grabbing someone's shoe! Why would you do that?!

Sneakiest Gladiator to referee
Legend's definitely one of the sneaky ones. On Collision, he'd sometimes go in a little higher than allowed. But the biggest rule breaker is Viper. He cheated on Duel and once on The Ring he would not let go of the contender!

DID YOU KNOW?

Sonia has amassed an impressive 123 international netball Test caps.

'When I used to play competitive sports, I used to hate it if the referees missed someone breaking a rule. I used to tell them off for it. But now I am one of the refs, I've become that person for the Gladiators.'

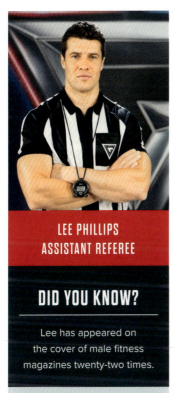

LEE PHILLIPS
ASSISTANT REFEREE

DID YOU KNOW?

Lee has appeared on the cover of male fitness magazines twenty-two times.

'During filming I got to have a go at The Eliminator, which was pretty cool. The Travelator moves a lot faster than it looks on TV!'

LEE

Lee is a former firefighter who has competed in the World Police and Fire Games, where he was crowned Ultimate Firefighter.

How I got the job

When the producers were casting the Gladiators for the series, they contacted me to design and run their fitness tests. At the tryouts, there were a lot of pull-up tests and things like that, in order to see where each of the potential Gladiators' strengths were. I did the same thing for the contenders, and after that they asked if I wanted to be one of the Referees. You don't get that sort of opportunity every day, so I thought, why not?

Challenges of the job

There are some events where Sonia and I can't get as stuck in as Mark. Like The Edge, for example – he's strapped in all the way up in the air, but we have to watch the event from a screen on the ground and it can be hard to see everything from there.

Toughest event

The Ring was tough because it was a new event and we needed to really tighten up the rules so that the contenders and Gladiators wouldn't find little loopholes to exploit. Gauntlet can get a bit fraught, too. Both the Gladiators and the contenders tend to push the boundaries a bit.

Sneakiest Gladiator to referee

Viper, obviously. He's a bit of a naughty boy, isn't he? We can't let him get away with anything. The rules are the rules, no matter who you are.

GLADIATORS ON GLADIATORS

As we have learned, the Gladiators are a tight-knit bunch. Even though they're a group of sixteen elite athletes who are all extremely used to being the best in their field, they managed to leave their competitive nature at the door and come together as one. There isn't an ego among them (well, apart from Legend). They're one big happy family, they claim.

But can that truly be the case? Are there really no rivalries within the group? There's only one way to find out: ask every Gladiator the same nine questions about the other Gladiators and see if any patterns emerge. Who's the worst loser of the group? Who's the biggest gossip? Who's the most annoying Gladiator?

Their answers to this highly scientific test are all profoundly revealing. Most of the male Gladiators nominated themselves as the toughest to beat on Duel (compared to none of the females), and one Gladiator clearly stands out as the most annoying!

Which Gladiator are you closest with?

STEEL 'Giant.'

SABRE 'Apollo.'

NITRO 'Viper. I understand Viper. I'm like the Viper tamer.'

FIRE 'Phantom.'

FURY 'Nitro.'

APOLLO 'Sabre.'

ATHENA 'Nitro.'

ELECTRO 'Comet.'

DYNAMITE 'Diamond.'

DIAMOND 'My little Dynamite.'

BIONIC 'Phantom. When we're together it's a proper vibe.'

VIPER 'Nitro.'

COMET 'Electro.'

LEGEND 'Nitro. Did he say me? No? That little rat.'

GIANT 'Steel.'

PHANTOM 'Fire.'

Most annoying Gladiator:

STEEL 'Legend.'

SABRE 'Legend.'

NITRO 'Legend.'

FIRE 'Legend.'

FURY 'Legend.'

APOLLO 'Legend.'

ATHENA 'Legend.'

ELECTRO 'Legend.'

DYNAMITE 'Legend.'

DIAMOND 'Legend.'

BIONIC 'Legend.'

VIPER 'Legend.'

COMET 'Legend.'

LEGEND 'Ha! Jealousy is an ugly emotion. Anyway, my answer is Steel.'

GIANT 'Legend.'

PHANTOM 'Legend.'

Gladiator you'd least like to do a Duel against:

STEEL 'Giant.'

SABRE 'Fire.'

NITRO 'Nitro.'

FIRE 'Dynamite. She's strong.'

FURY 'Sabre.'

APOLLO 'Apollo.'

ATHENA 'Giant.'

ELECTRO 'Giant.'

DYNAMITE 'Bionic.'

DIAMOND 'Bionic.'

BIONIC 'Bionic.'

VIPER 'Giant.'

COMET 'Giant, obviously.'

LEGEND 'Legend.'

GIANT 'Phantom is the only person to have ever beaten me in Duel, but I'm going to get my own back.'

PHANTOM (after twenty seconds of silence): 'Bionic.'

Weirdest Gladiator:

STEEL 'Diamond. I don't think she'd even tried coffee before the show.'

SABRE 'Phantom. He's well weird. Have you seen his Instagram? Weird, man.'

NITRO 'Phantom.'

FIRE 'Viper.'

FURY 'Diamond.'

APOLLO 'Dynamite.'

'I understand Viper.
I'm like the Viper tamer.'
NITRO

ATHENA '**Diamond**.'

ELECTRO '**Nitro** – how can someone be so energetic?!'

DYNAMITE 'Probably me.'

DIAMOND '**Comet**. She puts ketchup on her roast dinners.'

BIONIC '**Viper**. He doesn't speak a lot, does he?'

VIPER '**Legend**.'

COMET 'I'm going to have to say me. I just really like ketchup, OK?'

LEGEND '**Viper**.'

GIANT '**Apollo**. He doesn't look like he should be as strong as he is. That's really weird.'

PHANTOM '**Legend**.'

Funniest Gladiator:

STEEL '**Legend**.'

SABRE '**Nitro**.'

NITRO '**Dynamite**.'

FIRE '**Legend**.'

FURY '**Legend**.'

APOLLO '**Legend**. I hate that I've put his name so many times.'

ATHENA '**Nitro**.'

ELECTRO '**Legend**.'

DYNAMITE '**Electro**.'

DIAMOND '**Fire**. She's hilarious.'

BIONIC 'I'll probably say **Legend**, because he just plays practical jokes 24/7.'

VIPER '**Nitro**.'

COMET '**Nitro**.'

LEGEND '**Steel**.'

GIANT '**Viper**. He is so angry all the time!'

PHANTOM '**Electro**.'

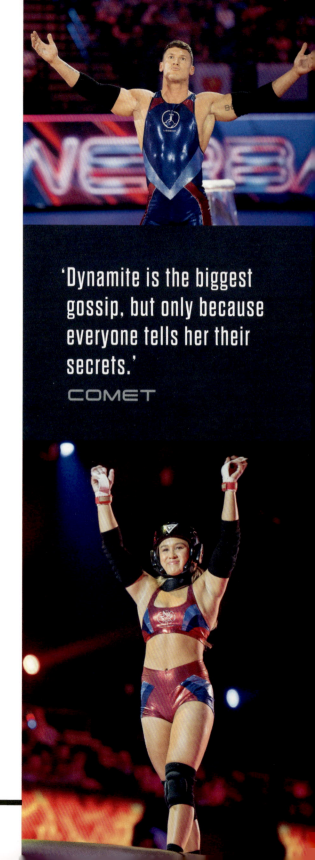

'Dynamite is the biggest gossip, but only because everyone tells her their secrets.'
COMET

Vainest Gladiator:

STEEL 'Legend.'

SABRE 'Me. I'm pretty vain.'

NITRO 'Sabre.'

FIRE 'Bionic.'

FURY 'Legend.'

APOLLO 'Legend.'

ATHENA 'Legend.'

ELECTRO 'Legend.'

DYNAMITE 'Legend.'

DIAMOND 'Legend, of course. He loves himself.'

BIONIC 'Legend.'

VIPER 'Legend.'

COMET 'Legend.'

LEGEND 'Oh fine, I'll say me as well then.'

GIANT 'Legend.'

PHANTOM 'Legend.'

Worst loser:

STEEL 'Viper. He does not take losing well.'

SABRE 'Diamond. She's a sister to me, but a nightmare at losing.'

NITRO 'Viper.'

FIRE 'Diamond. She's intense, man.'

FURY 'Viper.'

APOLLO 'Definitely Diamond.'

ATHENA 'Viper.'

ELECTRO 'Viper.'

DYNAMITE 'Viper.'

DIAMOND 'Viper and me!'

BIONIC 'Diamond. She'll shout at me for that.'

VIPER 'Legend.'

COMET '**Diamond**. She threw someone's shoe!'

LEGEND '**Diamond**. Anyone who didn't say Diamond has bottled it.'

GIANT '**Viper**.'

PHANTOM '**Viper**.'

Biggest gossip:

STEEL '**Dynamite**.'

SABRE '**Bionic**.'

NITRO 'None of us.'

FIRE 'Nobody's a gossip, but maybe **Sabre**.'

FURY '**Fire**.'

APOLLO '**Fire**.'

ATHENA '**Sabre**.'

ELECTRO 'I can't answer that!'

DYNAMITE '**Sabre**.'

DIAMOND '**Viper!**'

BIONIC '**Sabre**, without a doubt.'

VIPER '**Sabre**.'

COMET '**Dynamite**, but only because everyone tells her their secrets.'

LEGEND '**Sabre's** a good gossip.'

GIANT '**Sabre**.'

PHANTOM 'No comment. Everyone's said Sabre? Still no comment!'

Least punctual Gladiator:

STEEL '**Phantom**.'

SABRE '**Apollo**.'

NITRO '**Apollo's** pretty bad.'

FIRE '**Apollo**.'

FURY '**Apollo**.'

APOLLO 'Me.'

ATHENA '**Legend**.'

ELECTRO '**Phantom**.'

DYNAMITE '**Nitro**.'

DIAMOND '**Nitro**.'

BIONIC '**Apollo's** always the last one ready.'

VIPER '**Apollo**.'

COMET '**Phantom**.'

LEGEND '**Phantom** is late all the time.'

GIANT '**Phantom**. That man would be late for his own funeral.'

PHANTOM 'None of us.'

MEET THE GLADIATOR

STATS

HEIGHT: **6 ft 5 in**

ARM LENGTH: **76cm**

THIGH: **70cm**

'You can't hide from me.
Like a Phantom in the night,
I will catch you.'

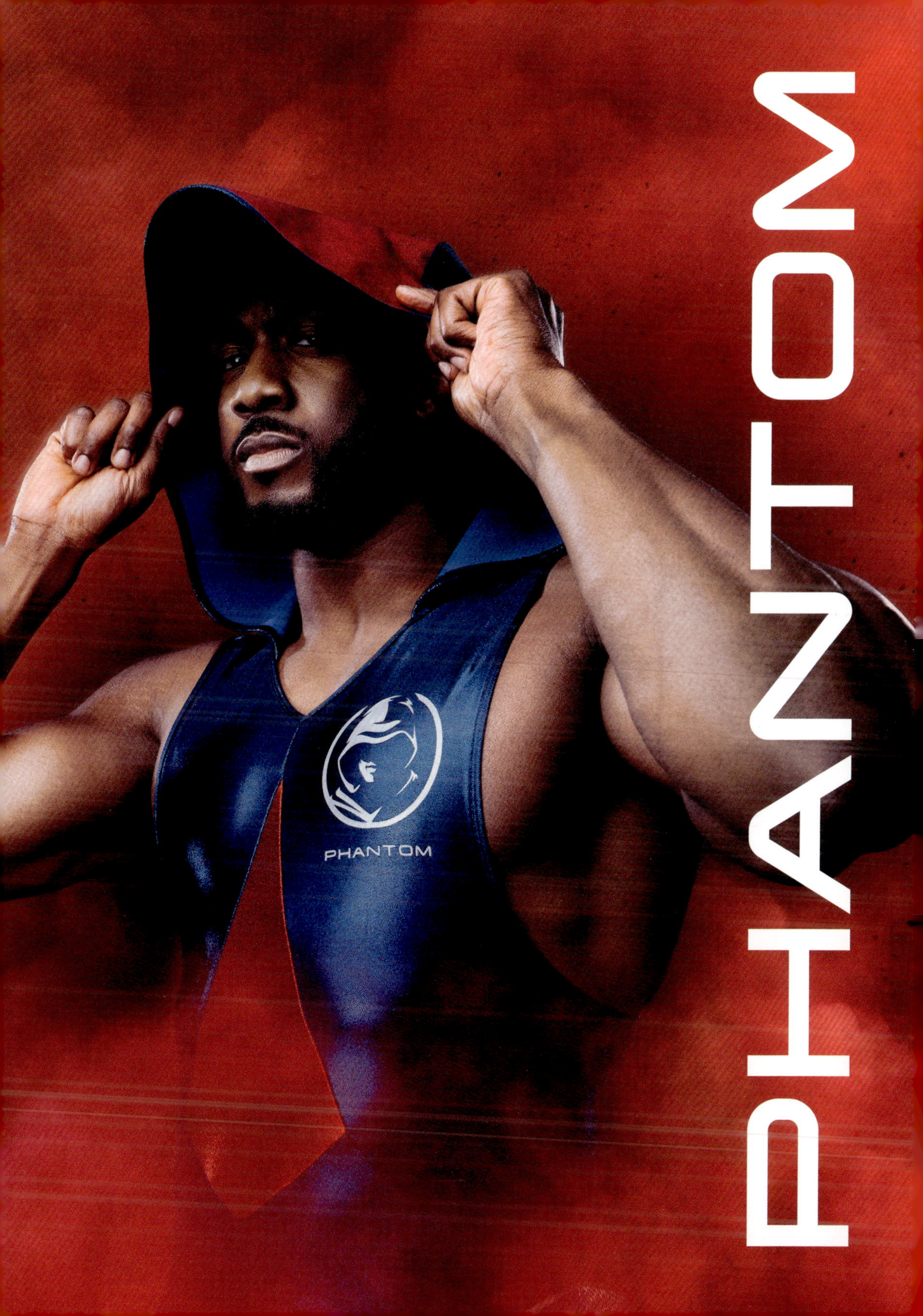
PHANTOM
PHANTOM

INTRODUCING PHANTOM

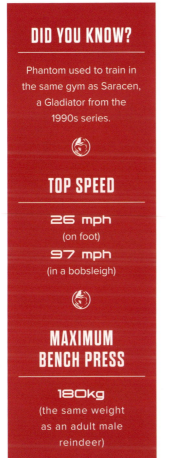

DID YOU KNOW?

Phantom used to train in the same gym as Saracen, a Gladiator from the 1990s series.

TOP SPEED

26 mph
(on foot)

97 mph
(in a bobsleigh)

MAXIMUM BENCH PRESS

180kg
(the same weight as an adult male reindeer)

When Phantom appears in the *Gladiators* arena, his face is hidden by a hood. This is because the man is a total enigma, our man of mystery. He comes and goes as he pleases. Nobody knows what he's thinking, or what he's going to do next.

But Phantom is able to use these qualities for good on *Gladiators*, outsmarting any contender who has the guts to face him.

He is also one of the fastest Gladiators, having represented Great Britain in the 2018 Winter Olympics as part of a four-man bobsledding team. In fact, the same year, Phantom's team reached the fastest speed ever recorded on a bobsleigh.

ABOUT ME

The Phantom way

I'm always ready for a showdown. I'll appear when you least expect it, and I won't give you an inch. But at the end of the day, if I see you giving your best, we can still be friends.

My workout routine

My motto is, train every day until you're exhausted, then take the day off and go again tomorrow.

What I eat

Cake for breakfast. That's a Phantom thing and it's going to be a Phantom thing forever. For dinner I'll usually eat chicken and broccoli, but breakfast has to be the most indulgent meal of the day. For me, that's birthday cake. Birthday cake is the opposite of my kryptonite. Even if it's not my birthday, I still sing 'Happy Birthday' to myself every morning. You've got birthday cake? Bring it on.

Growing up

I did really well academically at school. I tried as hard as I could, because I needed a scholarship to get into university. When I was at uni, I found track and field, which has been great for me. It all comes from hard work.

What I'm like in real life

Growing up, I threw myself into sport. I was too busy playing tennis or badminton or football after school to get into too much trouble, which really helped as there was a lot of that going on around me on the council estate I was raised on.

My favourite event on *Gladiators* …

I love Duel, because it's man vs man. You get to stare into the contender's eyes and you can really see what they're made of. Some are shaken up. Some give it back. One contender started hitting his helmet before the event began to get into the zone. But I've never lost. We've had some really strong contenders, but they don't move me.

… and my least favourite

Gauntlet. The pads are really annoying. The ones that you wear like huge gloves leave you in a vulnerable position, and they don't let you hit people as hard as you'd like.

My journey

I was initially a sprinter but took up bobsledding after I was approached to do some trials in my mid-twenties. Bobsledding involves being away from the UK for five months of the year, so you need funds behind you, and trying to raise them was hard. But I did and those were the four craziest years of my life. It was so competitive that I couldn't take my foot off the pedal.

My hero

My mum. We've clashed a lot. I always tell her that we're not friends, but she's the best mum I could have asked for. She helped me develop my moral backbone, and she gave me a code of conduct, which I've kept for the whole of my life. But she's also been an inspiration in the things she's had to overcome, and she did it all with four kids.

What I've learned

The Gladiators are sixteen competitive, highly driven individuals, but we literally get on like family. During school and my bobsleigh career there were always personality clashes, but there have been none on the show. Absolutely none. Kudos to the production staff, because they've created a support unit where you don't ever feel alone in any circumstance. We have created a really special *Gladiators* bubble, and it means that there's no ego between us. I mean, it's still early days, but fingers crossed!

GET THE LOOK

Just get your favourite hoodie out! I want as many people doing Phantom impressions as possible.

COMET

WALK-OUT MOVE

STEP 01 Cartwheel out.

STEP 02 Kick one leg out in a circle in front of you, as high and as wide as you can.

STEP 03 Put one hand on your hip, raise the other hand high above your head and dip your knee.

STEP 04 Smile confidently.

ALTERNATIVE POSE

Kick one leg up and out like a ballet dancer, while keeping your arms straight out and back.

'You've got to be flexible and fearless to do my moves.'

APOLLO

'I love my ancient statue pose. But the one that gets the most attention is my "bring it on" move.'

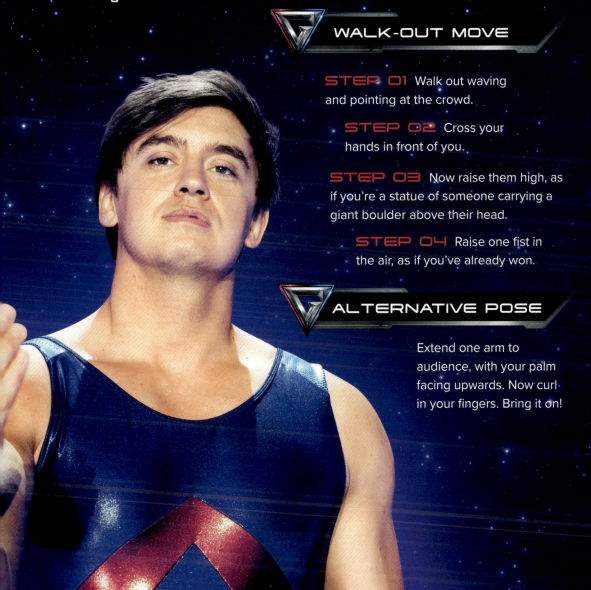

WALK-OUT MOVE

STEP 01 Walk out waving and pointing at the crowd.

STEP 02 Cross your hands in front of you.

STEP 03 Now raise them high, as if you're a statue of someone carrying a giant boulder above their head.

STEP 04 Raise one fist in the air, as if you've already won.

ALTERNATIVE POSE

Extend one arm to audience, with your palm facing upwards. Now curl in your fingers. Bring it on!

PHANTOM

'I love the hood.
You gotta
keep things
mysterious!'

 ## WALK-OUT MOVE

STEP 01 Walk out slowly and enigmatically with your hood up and your head down.

STEP 02 Cross your hands in front of you.

STEP 03 Now bring them down and out diagonally and point your fingers, while you drop to one knee.

STEP 04 Slowly and dramatically pull back the hood to reveal your face.

STEP 05 Point at the audience with both hands.

 ## ALTERNATIVE POSE

Put your hood up. Now slowly remove it.

ATHENA

'The trick to my move is to carry yourself with grace and confidence.'

WALK-OUT MOVE

STEP 01 Strut out with two arms raised wide above your head.

STEP 02 Now confidently flick them down to your waist.

STEP 03 Turn to the side and stretch one arm out in front of you, as if it's a bow.

STEP 04 Use the same hand to pull back an imaginary arrow on the bow, like you're about to fire it.

STEP 05 Release with a flourish.

ALTERNATIVE POSE

Just fire an invisible bow and arrow.

ELECTRO

'My moves are all really fast.
I'm a speedy girl.'

 WALK-OUT MOVE

STEP 01 Walk out with one hand raised above your head.

STEP 02 Bring the hand down to your waist and then flick it out to the side.

STEP 03 Cross your hands in front of your body.

STEP 04 Take one of your hands and hold it out in front of you, like you're trying to blast your audience with a lightning bolt.

 ALTERNATIVE POSE

Elbows into your side, lower arms outstretched, as if you're conducting electricity through your hands.

DYNAMITE

'My move is pretty easy but that just means lots of people can do it.'

WALK-OUT MOVE

STEP 01 Run out waving. You are young and full of energy.

STEP 02 Make your hands into fists and then put them on your hips.

STEP 03 Now smile!

ALTERNATIVE POSE

As above, but without running anywhere.

DIAMOND

'Stand tall. Make yourself shine as bright as you can.'

WALK-OUT MOVE

STEP 01 Walk out slowly and confidently, like you're on a catwalk.

STEP 02 Stop, and put your hands on your hips, making sure to show off your muscles.

STEP 03 Flip your hair and walk forwards.

STEP 04 Make a diamond by crossing your wrists and then bending your hands back until the fingertips touch.

STEP 05 Blow a kiss with both hands.

ALTERNATIVE POSE

Place an invisible crown on your head, flexing your shoulders and arms as you do.

BIONIC

'Keeping your head down is key. You've got to look like you mean to win.'

WALK-OUT MOVE

STEP 01 Walk out with your head down. Now stop.

STEP 02 Drop your hands in front of you.

STEP 03 Slowly but powerfully, raise one arm up to shoulder height.

STEP 04 Do the same with the other arm.

STEP 05 In one robotic movement, twist to the side, raise the back arm into a bicep curl and the front arm in front of you.

ALTERNATIVE POSE

Flex one bicep and outstretch the other arm.

MEET THE GLADIATOR

STATS

HEIGHT: **5 ft 8 in**
ARM LENGTH: **58cm**
KEY SKILL: **Reactions**

'Contenders, watch out
for my electric-fast reactions.
You're in for a shock!'

ELECTRO

INTRODUCING ELECTRO

DID YOU KNOW?

One of Electro's favourite meals is chicken and jam. 'Don't knock it until you've tried it.'

WINGSPAN

175cm
(the same as Comet's height)

MAXIMUM SQUAT

twenty reps in a row
100kg
(the same weight as ten watermelons)

The Gladiators are a group of huge personalities, so Electro might not be the one you notice at first. She isn't as loud or flashy as the others. She doesn't follow the crowd. She's effortlessly cool, calm and collected.

But don't let this coolness fool you. Just because she's more reserved, it doesn't mean that she isn't paying attention. Instead, she's just waiting for contenders to slip up, and that's when she'll pounce. Electro's reaction times are second to none – once a sprinter, Electro was one of the fastest around, and as a bodybuilder she was one of the strongest.

Gladiators is her chance to show the world what a dangerous combination that is.

ABOUT ME

The Electro way

I'm cool, calm, collected. In the events I've got my Terminator game face on. Once it's over, I'll be a bit more jokey again.

My workout routine

Bodybuilding is my background, so I still like to include that element, but now I add the conditioning element of CrossFit too. I like working out in a way that boosts my physique, but I also like to work on my speed and agility and so on. With bodybuilding, you look good but you're not always actually very functionally fit, so combining both those elements is really key for me.

What I eat

I have a really high-calorie diet. I don't track my diet as much as I did when I was bodybuilding. Now I'm a lot more free, especially with this style of training where you can eat more and still maintain a leaner physique. I definitely like to eat clean, because I just feel better that way, but I eat all the foods that everyone else likes to eat as well. Pretty basic really!

Growing up

I loved school, to be fair. I just thought that it was good banter. I always did sports at lunchtimes and in clubs. I was still very into education as well, and got good grades, but obviously alongside lots of sports. I'd rather go to school than sit at home. I had 100 per cent attendance because I never get sick.

What I'm like in real life

I started as a sprinter. That began at school; I was the unbeaten champ. When I was ten, I watched the 2008 Olympics and saw Usain Bolt, and I got my mum to take me to a local athletics track the next week. I remember my coach saying to my mum that he didn't think I was serious, so I made sure I won my first competition. After that he was like, 'OK, cool.' Obviously, as you get older, the competition becomes tougher, and you get your first loss. But that's good, because it makes you focus. Hard work beats talent when talent doesn't work hard.

My favourite event on *Gladiators* ...

I love Powerball. I love the contact of it. You can just take people down. It's a super-fast pace, too. It's only a minute long, but it feels like it goes on for ages.

... and my least favourite

None. Every event has its place, and I couldn't imagine one event not being there.

My journey

Like everyone, there are things that I've gone through in life, but sport has always grounded me. It's what I've always been naturally good at. If there has been a period of my life where something's happened and I couldn't train, I don't feel 100 per cent myself. But as soon as I start again, I realise that sport is the gift I've been given. Once I tap into that, I'm right back on track.

My hero

With sprinting, obviously, Usain Bolt. And then similarly, for bodybuilding, there were a couple of girls that I found on Instagram where I was like, 'OK, cool, you're inspiring me, I'm gonna go down that path.' Same with CrossFit, and just life in general. There are definitely things you can learn from everyone. Everyone's an inspiration to me in some way.

GET THE LOOK

In terms of my make-up, I've got electric blue eyeliner and a bit of eyeshadow. I always love to be different. Glossy lips, too. My lips will never be ready without gloss. My outfit has long mesh sleeves, to be different again. I really like standing out from the crowd. As for my facial expression, you can't really tell what I'm thinking. It's hard to judge what I'm going to do. Game face on.

What I've learned

I've always believed that you've got the ability to do anything. It's always about mindset. You're not going to succeed if you haven't got the mindset to go with it. Before *Gladiators*, I'd always participated in solo sports, so I've also learned that I like to have a team around me.

BEHIND THE SCENES

If you think that *Gladiators* looks like a big show on TV, just wait until you see it in the flesh. Putting on a show on this scale requires a massive operation, with dozens of different departments all working around the clock to make the experience the best it can possibly be for everyone. Every detail is meticulously planned and executed. It's a staggeringly huge job.

Practice makes perfect

As Series Editor, Reshmi Bajnath is basically in charge of overseeing the whole operation. She is involved in every decision, from the graphic fonts used for the clocks during the events, to deciding which Gladiators will participate in which event. 'Yeah, it's a big job, but I absolutely love it,' she says. 'It's a rare privilege to work on such an iconic show that I watched and loved as a child.'

Long before any spectators enter the Utilita Arena Sheffield, Reshmi works with the rest of the team to organise rehearsals to make sure everything looks as good as it can. 'We spend four or five days practising and rehearsing every event,' she says. This requires every department of production. 'Cameras, lighting, music, sound. The rehearsals are our first opportunity to see how everything looks onscreen. Are the shots looking good? Are the floor projections looking the way we want? What do we need to change? It's also the first chance we get to see how long it takes to set an event up and take it down afterwards. The rehearsals are really important to us.'

As the woman in charge, Reshmi is clear that making *Gladiators* is a big team effort. 'We all work really closely, and we all work extremely hard, but this is also the most fun show to work on. It's such a unique environment because we're filming in front of thousands of people. It doesn't matter that it's long days, or that it can be tough, everyone is just so happy to be making the show.' What's more, she's already thinking of ways to make *Gladiators* even better for the 2025 series. 'We've got loads of really exciting new things lined up,' she says. 'Lots of big surprises!'

From school to screen

Libby McInnes is an Assistant Producer on the show, working in the Events Team. That means that she played an important role in developing and testing the two new events for the 2024 series, The Ring and The Edge. 'The Edge originally had a working title of The Hive,' she reveals. 'It took hours and hours to test. At first, we laid out the design of the event with tape on the floor, but we had to be extremely precise about the size and angle. It tested OK, but there wasn't that huge drop that there is on the show, so it didn't have very much jeopardy.'

So the next time the team tested it, they went to a school in Glasgow and laid out the design with long wooden school benches. 'That gave us more of a sense of how it would be off the ground, because it made it a bit harder for the players to cut corners. Seeing how spectacular The Edge looks on the show, with all the effects and

lights, is extremely gratifying, especially knowing how basic the first few tests were.'

When Libby and the Events Team test events, one of their main roles is to try to figure out all the different ways that contenders might cheat while playing them. 'The people who come on the show are so competitive, and some like to look for ways to get an advantage,' Libby says. 'On The Wall, having loosely tied shoes was an issue, but apparently back in the 1990s series, contenders used to grease their legs so that the Gladiators couldn't grab on to them!' She says that talking through every event in enormous detail with the Producers and the Referees so everyone is really clear about what is and isn't allowed is the best way to catch anyone bending the rules. But Libby says she also tries to see how far she can bend the rules herself. 'I've got nine brothers and sisters,' she laughs. 'So I'm used to people pushing the limits to see what they can get away with!'

Building the dream

Damian Weymouth is in charge of rigging the show. 'Basically, if it's hanging off the roof, we've looked after it in one form or another,' he explains. The roof of the arena plays a very important part of *Gladiators*. As well as the lights, several event elements are stored up there for a quick set-up and are flown down onto the arena floor to play

– this includes the Hang Tough rig, The Edge and The Eliminator's Travelator.

'The weight of everything we use on the show is about 90 tons, and it fills several trucks,' Damian continues. 'I believe *Gladiators* is the heaviest show ever to have taken place at the Sheffield Arena. I'm pretty sure we beat the previous record, which was a Metallica tour.'

The events on *Gladiators* all need huge amounts of equipment to be assembled and pulled down as quickly and as smoothly as possible, on a regular basis, and this alone requires a vast amount of coordination. 'Different events take longer than others to set up,' explains Damian. 'Collision is quick to take down, but it's very time-consuming to set. It's bulky, it's

heavy, it's really intricate. There's a lot of it, and we have to be 100 per cent accurate in how we set it out. The Eliminator is a big one, too, but over the course of the 2024 series we managed to cut two thirds of the setting time.' The key to achieving this, like everything else on *Gladiators*, comes down to teamwork. 'My colleague coordinates the majority of the mats and rolling items, while I tend to do the flying items [the equipment that flies down onto the floor],' Damian says. 'Everyone knows what goes where and when it needs to go. It just helps with the flow.'

Revving up the crowd

Nevertheless, with all this heavy lifting to do, it can sometimes be up to forty-five minutes between one event ending and another beginning. That's a lot of time to fill, and with 3,000 people in the arena, it could be easy to let the energy drop. Which is where Stuart Holdham comes in. He's the *Gladiators* warm-up performer, and it's his job to keep everyone entertained between events.

'I always say that *Gladiators* is actually two shows,' he says. 'There's the show you see on TV, and the show you see when you come to see it live.' Stuart is unbelievably full of beans on the arena floor, playing games and telling jokes and changing into any one of his forty-two different costumes, while working with DJs Mylo and Rosie from a local radio station, who blast out a steady stream of pop songs.

'I get as much fun out of it as the audience does,' he says. 'We do a Mexican wave that the audience goes crazy for. We play something called Arena Ball, where we get a giant beach ball and try to bat it around the arena as quickly as possible. The record for a full lap at the moment is one minute and eighteen seconds. We do a Chocolate Biscuit Challenge with the dads, where they place a chocolate digestive on their forehead and try to get it into their mouth in record time, even though they usually end up with chocolate running down their eyelids. Plus we give prizes for the best banners as well.

'We even get a few chants going,' he continues. 'When Bradley and Barney come out, everyone goes "Oh, Bradley and Barney!" to the tune of "Seven Nation Army" by the White Stripes, whether they like it or not!'

Better still, Stuart often manages to get the Gladiators involved in his shenanigans. 'We always get a bunch of kids down onto the arena floor and make five of them do a tug of war against one Gladiator,' he says. 'It wouldn't be such smooth sailing without the Gladiators willing to help out.'

Stuart's job sounds exhausting. He works long hours to keep the crowds entertained, and one day he says that he walked 16,500 steps across the arena floor doing it. But it's worthwhile, because an entertained

'Legend does his own hair ... and as he keeps reminding us, he's perfect anyway.'
JACQUI

crowd is a supportive one. 'The support for our contenders is amazing,' he says. 'I remember one of the contenders saying, "If it wasn't for the audience, I'd have never got to the finishing line." Every single person in the audience supports them, and it's because we want the audience to feel special. They're such an important part of the show.'

Polishing perfection

Stuart is not the only one working long hours. On filming days, Jacqui Mallett and her team arrive very early to set up for *Gladiators* – because they're in charge of everyone's hair and make-up. 'There are eight of us in our team, and we're responsible for sixteen Gladiators, plus the four contenders and the three Referees,' she says. 'The theory is that we take two Gladiators each, but it doesn't always work that way because some take much longer to get ready than others.'

The Gladiator who takes the longest is Fury. 'My colleague Julie, who's basically my right-hand man, always does her hair,' explains Jacqui. 'Fury needs a long time because her hair is so elaborate. She has lots of braids, and bits of blue put in.' Usually hair as complicated as this requires the use of pins, but that's a no-go here because the Gladiators wear helmets and there's an injury risk.

'Part of our job is also topping up everyone's fake tan, because it can get rubbed off during events,' she explains. 'Giant takes the longest for that, just because there's so much of him! Sometimes a bunch of us have to take a limb each to get him done in time.' Meanwhile, Jacqui says that the easiest Gladiator to look after is probably Legend. 'He does his own hair, because he likes it a certain way,' she says. 'And also, as he keeps reminding us, he's perfect anyway.'

'This is honestly one of the happiest jobs I've ever done,' she continues. 'Everyone is so lovely to work with. The Gladiators are so encouraging and positive to each other. In fact, the hardest part of my job is probably trying to get them all to sit still. Once the music gets started in the room, they're impossible to wrangle!'

Shedding light

Another often-overlooked aspect of the show is its state-of-the-art lighting, which provides its own challenges. 'We use projectors, so we can beam images onto the walls and floor,' explains Nigel Catmur, who is in charge of lighting the show. 'It means we can use The Wall as a big screen when the Gladiators walk out, plus we're able to give all the events a different feel.' In total, Nigel uses eighteen projectors that cover the arena floor in a grid. 'Lining

them up is a very, very long and laborious process, that we have to do over several nights,' he says.

But, again, it's worth it. 'We build the projection in to almost every event,' he says. 'Without projection, The Ring wouldn't really exist. We've set it up so that the lighting interacts with the gameplay. Not only do the lights project the pitch onto the floor, but the floor pulses whenever a contender scores.' As well as all the projectors, Nigel says that the show uses over a thousand lights, including twelve spotlights, requiring several kilometres of cables to keep it all running.

'It's all to make everything as visually exciting as possible,' he says. 'And we learned so much in the 2024 series that the 2025 series is going to be even more spectacular!'

Catching it on camera

With such a visually stunning show, it's important everything is captured on screen. As the Director of *Gladiators*, it's the job of Chris Power to decide where to put all the cameras. 'It's a very big show to direct, and it's set in a huge arena, so the scale of it is enormous,' he says. 'We have thirteen cameras to cover everything, and we only get one chance. You have to make sure that you have every angle covered, in case something unexpected happens. When it does, it's my job to react to whatever is happening, and move the cameras into the right place to make sure the viewers see it.'

Making Chris's job harder is the fact that every event is different, and therefore needs to be shot differently. 'The Edge is a really challenging one, because it takes place thirty feet in the air,' he says.

'Originally, we tried to put four minicams up there on the structure, but everything shook so much that nobody could tell what was going on. But luckily we also had camera cranes that could just about stretch up high enough to film the event. The Eliminator is also really hard to film, especially when one contender is a long way behind the other. But part of my job is to plan for the unexpected.'

Of course, the unexpected also includes some of the more unpredictable Gladiators. 'At the end of the events, we try to follow the Gladiators as they move around the arena,' he says. 'But Viper really doesn't like it when we do it to him. If he's lost an event, or something has gone wrong for him, he'll literally try to knock the cameraperson over!'

Feeding the army

With so many people working on the show, it's important that everyone stays happy and fed. Enter Mark Bunce, the show's caterer. It's his job to offer a selection of lunch choices to the hundreds of people who make the show happen, all cooked in his restaurant-grade articulated truck. 'We arrive at the arena at six o'clock every morning and get cooking,' he explains, adding: 'We probably get through about 800 chicken breasts a week on *Gladiators*.'

But *Gladiators* is a unique show to cater for. Not only does Mark have to feed the crew, but also sixteen enormous athletes who need to be constantly ready for battle. 'The Gladiators usually want huge amounts of protein,' he says. 'That means lots of grilled chicken, lots of broccoli, lots of brown rice. It never looks particularly appetising compared to what everyone else gets to eat, but I'm not a professional athlete. They're such big units, the Gladiators. When they look at food, they're not even registering if it tastes nice or not. It's pure fuel to them.'

He continues: 'Sometimes the Gladiators come to me and say, "We've had chicken so many times! Could we change it up?" It's never a problem. I do sometimes see Comet loading industrial quantities of ketchup onto her food, though. I don't know where the protein is in that!'

You want to know the scale of *Gladiators*? We've barely touched the sides. As well as the riggers, caterers, lighting technicians and warm-up performers, there are medics, drivers, hairdressers, make-up artists, physiotherapists, editors, camera operators, sound recordists, producers and runners who are all just as dedicated to keeping the show going as anyone else. When the Gladiators say that they're a big family, remember that they're talking about all of these unseen people in the background, too.

MEET THE GLADIATOR

STATS

HEIGHT: **6 ft**
WINGSPAN: **186cm**
KEY SKILL: **Storming off**

'The contenders are hissss-tory.'

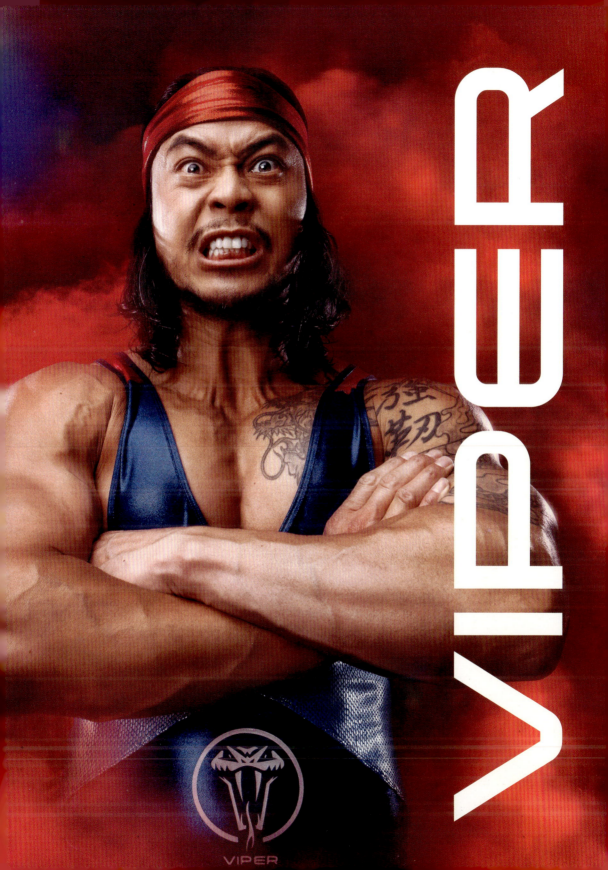

INTRODUCING VIPER

DID YOU KNOW?

Viper sometimes eats microphones in his post-event interviews. For the 2025 series, he's threatening to come for the audience.

MAXIMUM LEG PRESS

600kg
(heavier than a big horse)

MAXIMUM DEADLIFT

230kg
(the same weight as seventy-seven games consoles)

Less a Gladiator and more an unknowable force of nature, Viper is the *Gladiators* bad boy. He barely speaks, preferring instead to communicate in snarls and roars. He is prone to sudden bursts of temper.

Despite this, Viper remains popular with the public, even though the idea of being liked by people angers and terrifies him in equal measure.

ABOUT ME

Viper likes to do things differently,
as you'll see from the answers to the
following questions.

The Viper way
I do whatever I want. I'm Viper.

My workout routine
I train however I want.

What I eat
Whatever I want.

Growing up
I did whatever I wanted.

Favourite movie
Snakes on a Plane.

Favourite music
Anything by Whitesnake.

Favourite food and drink
Pancakessssss and
hissss-pressssso

My car
Ana-honda

Favourite wrestler
Jake 'The Snake' Roberts.

**Favourite Norwegian
handball team**
Vipers Kristiansand.

Favourite toy
Rattle.

Favourite kitchen equipment
Scales.

Favourite subject
Hisss-tory.

My favourite event on *Gladiators* ...
Any event where I smash
contenders.

... and my least favourite
The Eliminator. I can't smash
contenders on that.

My hero
Darth Vader.

What I've learned
Cheaters always prosper.

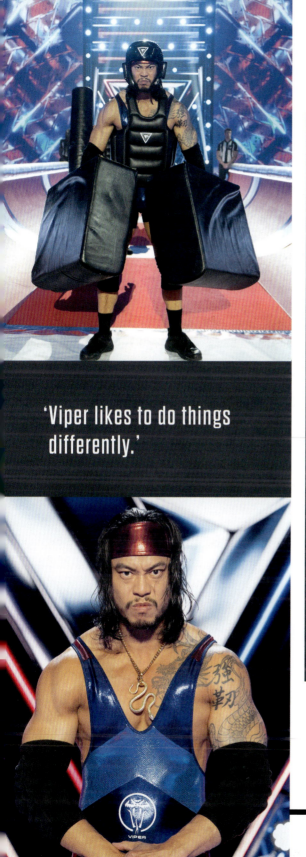

'Viper likes to do things differently.'

GET THE LOOK

Grow your hair long. Never wash it. Smash things up. Don't forget to snarl a lot.

Congratulations, you have now become Viper.

WHICH GLADIATOR ARE YOU?

The great thing about the Gladiators is that all have distinct personalities, so it's easy to find one you relate to the most. For instance, are you a level-headed older sibling type? Chances are you're a 'Steel'. Are you super-smart and strategic? You might be an 'Athena'. Are you always full of energy and love to do handstands? Congratulations, you're a 'Dynamite'.

But if you're struggling to figure out which Gladiator best represents your own specific personality type, don't worry. These fifteen questions will get right to the heart of what your strengths are, and which Gladiator is your true spirit animal.

01 **You pass a mirror. What is your first instinct?**

A   You give yourself the biggest smile imaginable.

B   You glare at it, to help you get your game face on.

C   You kiss your own reflection, because you can't believe how good-looking it is.

D   You practise a piercing stare, so that you can scare your opponents.

E   You don't have a reflection.

 02 **Your motto is ...**

A   'Good vibes all day.'

B   'Nothing will get in my way today.'

C   'I'm number one, so why try harder?'

D   'I'm unbreakable.'

E   An incomprehensible series of grunts and snarls

 03 **What do you like to do on your day off?**

A   I go outside and make friends with strangers.

B   I power down and recharge.

C   I go into a room decorated with pictures of me, and soak up the glory.

D   I polish my crown.

E   Destroy.

 04 **If you were a Gladiator, your favourite thing would be ...**

A   The roar of the crowds.

B   Getting to take down the contenders.

C   Showing everyone how incredible I am.

D   Inspiring the young people watching.

E   Eating Bradley Walsh's microphone.

 05 **When you visit a zoo, what's the first animal you look at?**

A   The chimpanzees, because they're sociable crowd pleasers.

B   The crocodiles. They're calm, but they can pounce.

C   The elephants, because they're the second biggest things there (after my ego).

D   The peacocks. They know how to put on a show.

E   The snakes, because we are genetically identical.

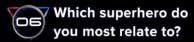 **06 Which superhero do you most relate to?**

A Someone bright and colourful, like Superman.

B Someone cool and powerful like Storm.

C Iron Man, a film about an arrogant idiot who pushes all his loved ones away.

D Wonder Woman.

E Imagine if Dracula bit Godzilla's neck during a zombie invasion. That.

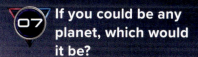 **07 If you could be any planet, which would it be?**

A Earth, because that's where all the people are.

B Neptune. It's distant but has amazing-looking electrical storms.

C The sun, because everything revolves around me. I know it's not a planet. I don't care.

D Saturn. It has the best accessories.

E Venus – it's deadly.

 08 What's your biggest talent?

A I'm an amazing dancer.

B I'm unreadable. I keep my emotions hidden.

C Are you suggesting there's a part of me that isn't talented? This is outrageous.

D I always give my best, no matter what.

E Snarling.

 09 And what's your worst quality?

A Sometimes I can be a bit too much for some people.

B I take my time before becoming your friend.

C I don't understand the question.

D I can get annoyed if I don't win.

E Cheating.

 10 If you could visit any moment in human history, when would it be?

A The 1970s.

B The 1980s.

C The moment of my birth, so I could witness all the doctors and nurses crying with gratitude at the gift of my existence.

D The 1990s.

E Now. Snakes live in the present.

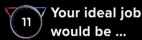
11 **Your ideal job would be …**

A   A children's entertainer.
B   A law enforcement officer.
C   The president of my own fan club.
D   A pop star.
E   A volcano.

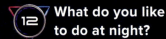
12 **What do you like to do at night?**

A   Invite people over and have a party.
B   Get an early night, because tomorrow it begins again.
C   I watch videos of myself, while cuddling a pillow that has my face on it.
D   I love going out with my friends to eat.
E   I don't sleep. I lie in wait.

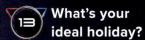
13 **What's your ideal holiday?**

A   Somewhere nice and sunny.
B   Somewhere cool.
C   Wherever I'll look the best – which is everywhere.
D   It doesn't matter, so long as I'm with my friends.
E   My secret lair hidden beneath the desert.

14 **It's your cheat day. What are you going to eat?**

A   A cake that I baked myself.
B   Chicken and broccoli. No days off, ever.
C   I will lick a picture of my own face.
D   I just love pizza!
E   Microphones.

15 **What's the first thing you will do after completing this quiz?**

A   I'll text my friends to see if they agree with the result.
B   I'll just read whatever is on the next page.
C   I'll disagree with the result, because none of the Gladiators are as perfect as me.
D   I'll share the results on Instagram.
E   I'll get angry about it.

RESULTS

Time to tot up your answers and find out which Gladiator represents you best (for more answers, see over the page).

 ATHENA
 COMET
 DIAMOND
 DYNAMITE

 ELECTRO
 FIRE
 FURY
SABRE

 APOLLO
 BIONIC
 GIANT
 LEGEND

 NITRO
PHANTOM
 STEEL
 VIPER

YOU ARE
NITRO

Congratulations! This result means that you are full of energy and the life and soul of the party. You know how to have a good time but, more importantly, you know how to make everyone else have a good time, too. What a pleasure you are to be around.

MOSTLY B'S

YOU ARE
ELECTRO

Congratulations! As super-cool as you are, you are all about business. You don't waste too much time being silly, but the important thing is that you'll get the job done, no matter what. You are a credit to any team you are part of.

MOSTLY C'S

YOU ARE
LEGEND

Congratulations! You have an ego so colossal that it could block out the sun. There is only one person in your world at any time, and that is you. You are the most skilled. You are the best looking. You are nothing less than perfection itself. Yes, this means that you're often annoying to be around, but who cares what anyone else thinks?

YOU ARE
DIAMOND

Congratulations! You have an exceptionally advanced sense of self. You know what you want, and you know how to get it, but that isn't going to stop you from having fun and being a good sport in the process. Like a diamond itself, you are strong and unbreakable.

YOU ARE
VIPER

Congratulations! You are an unknowable enigma, a pure malevolent force. Are you human? Serpent? Nobody knows. All that's important is that you are absolutely terrifying.

MEET THE GLADIATOR

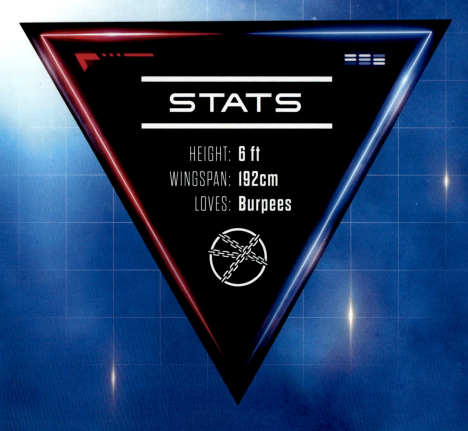

STATS

HEIGHT: **6 ft**
WINGSPAN: **192cm**
LOVES: **Burpees**

'If a contender manages to beat me,
they obviously worked very hard.
They deserve that win.'

STEEL

INTRODUCING STEEL

DID YOU KNOW?

Steel once won the title of 'UK's Fittest Man'.

MAXIMUM HANDSTAND WALK

90m
(longer than seven double-decker buses)

MAXIMUM NUMBER OF BURPEES IN A ROW

778
(which is legitimately hellish)

Steel carries himself with the ease of someone who knows exactly how good they are.

In the moments before facing a contender, when other Gladiators are snarling and staring and psyching themselves up, you'll find Steel smiling and joking. This is because he understands exactly what an impossible opponent he is.

Steel has spent his entire adult life in pursuit of greatness. He knows that he's put in more hours than you, and he knows he can probably run faster and hit harder, too. So what's the use in getting into a flap about it?

ABOUT ME

The Steel way

I'm Mr Nice Guy. You'll always see me smiling, very happy. On the rare occasion that contenders beat me, I'll always congratulate them. I'm gracious in both defeat and victory. But that doesn't mean I don't mean business.

My workout routine

I train twice a day, for three to four hours, six days a week. If I'm doing cardio it could be sprints or longer endurance runs. But then there are CrossFit workouts, and weightlifting and gymnastics. Now I also do things like rock climbing and rugby, too.

What I eat

I eat a huge amount: 4,000 calories a day. I'll get my main source of protein from a combination of chicken, steak and salmon. My carbs come from rice, potato and oats. And then I get loads of veggies and fats from things like avocado and pumpkin seeds. I have one cheat day a week where I literally eat anything, but it's usually doughnuts and pizza.

Growing up

I was very, very different to how I am now. I was overweight as a kid, and lacked a lot of confidence. I was extremely self-conscious: I remember multiple times when I used to miss school because there were swimming lessons and I didn't want to take my top off in front of the other kids. I ate a lot of junk food and didn't like the way I looked.

What I'm like in real life

I found CrossFit when I was twenty-four. But six feet tall and 100-odd kilos is not an ideal weight or height for CrossFit competitions. Ideally, you'd want to be small, because you can do everything quicker if you're more compact. During my first competition, some guy said to me, 'You're way too big to ever get anywhere in this sport.' I've spent my entire career trying to prove him wrong. And I did, because eventually I became the UK's Fittest Man.

My favourite event on Gladiators ...

I always thought that my favourite would be Hang Tough, because I spend a lot of time training on the rings. But my actual favourite has turned out to be The Ring. I always wanted to be a professional rugby player when I was younger, but I had to let that dream go after an injury. But The Ring is just a one-minute-long rugby tackling match. I'd forgotten how much I really love tackling people.

... and my least favourite

I'm an all-rounder. I'll have a go at anything.

My journey

During my low days at school, my dad sat me down and said, 'Look, I can tell you're unhappy in how you look. And I know you want a new computer console. If we sort your nutrition out and you stick to the plan for a couple months, we'll get it for you.' That was the catalyst for my fitness journey. I started eating less junk food, less chocolate, and soon I started losing weight and feeling better about myself. Within a couple of years I went from being the kid who was overweight to the kid who was into fitness. And then when I left school I became a trainer, because I wanted to help as many other people as I could on their own fitness journeys. My mission on *Gladiators* is to inspire the next generation of kids who are watching the show. I hope my story will show that anything's possible if you work hard.

My hero

I love Michael Jordan, for his dominance in sport. And Usain Bolt is an idol, because he could be two minutes away from running the biggest race of his life

GET THE LOOK

First of all, have a big smile on your face. Be friendly, have positive chats. And I've got two moves. One is where I scream and go to rip my shirt, and the other is following that up with crossed arms and, most importantly, a smile.

at the Olympics and he's still smiling and waving to the crowd. More importantly, there's my mum and dad, just because of their work ethic. They've given me a great life.

What I've learned

So many people have contacted me to tell me how much my story has inspired them. It made me realise how much I enjoy helping people get in shape and achieve their goals.

PUMP-UP PLAYLIST

APOLLO

WALK-OUT MUSIC

Lenny Kravitz, 'Are You Gonna Go My Way'

PUMP-UP MUSIC

I think deep down in my core I'm probably a bit of a rocker. Red Hot Chili Peppers, Arctic Monkeys, even some of the old eighties and nineties bands like Kiss or Mötley Crüe or AC/DC. Basically, anything with a guitar riff and some cool vocals in it.

FIRE

WALK-OUT MUSIC

Celeste, 'Stop This Flame' (Remix)

PUMP-UP MUSIC

I listen to a lot of female-inspired rap, so there's a lot of black female empowerment. Nicki Minaj is my favourite, but I also like Lady Leshurr when I want to keep it UK too.

DYNAMITE

WALK-OUT MUSIC

Jessie J ft. Ariana Grande and Nicki Minaj, 'Bang Bang'

PUMP-UP MUSIC

I like high-energy pop tunes and really aggressive music. So it's Eminem and AC/DC, but all the Girl Power playlists too.

LEGEND

WALK-OUT MUSIC

Tina Turner, 'Simply the Best'

PUMP-UP MUSIC

My favourite genre would probably be my own music. Like I do actually write and record my own music, and I play instruments as well. It's very, very inspiring. My favourite songs of mine are 'Wow, I'm Great', 'I Love My Hair', 'I'm Better Than You' and 'Everyone Stop Asking for My Autograph (I've Got Things to Do)'.

FURY

WALK-OUT MUSIC

Ed Sheeran ft. Bring Me The Horizon, '**Bad Habits**'

PUMP-UP MUSIC

My cochlear implant allows me to experience music despite being profoundly deaf in both ears. The processor sits on the outside of my ear, so I can only use headphones that sit over them. My favourite songs to get me pumped up are '**Jungle**' by X Ambassadors and Jamie N Commons (ft. Jay Z), '**Rise**' by Katy Perry, '**The Spectre**' by Alan Walker and '**I Like the Way You Move**' by X-Terra.

GIANT

WALK-OUT MUSIC

Rag'n'Bone Man, **'Giant'**

PUMP-UP MUSIC

I like to train to songs with big emotions, so I can transfer the emotions into my workout. At the moment I really like the soundtrack to *A Star Is Born*. **'Shallow'** is the big song from that, but there's one at the end that gets me every time.

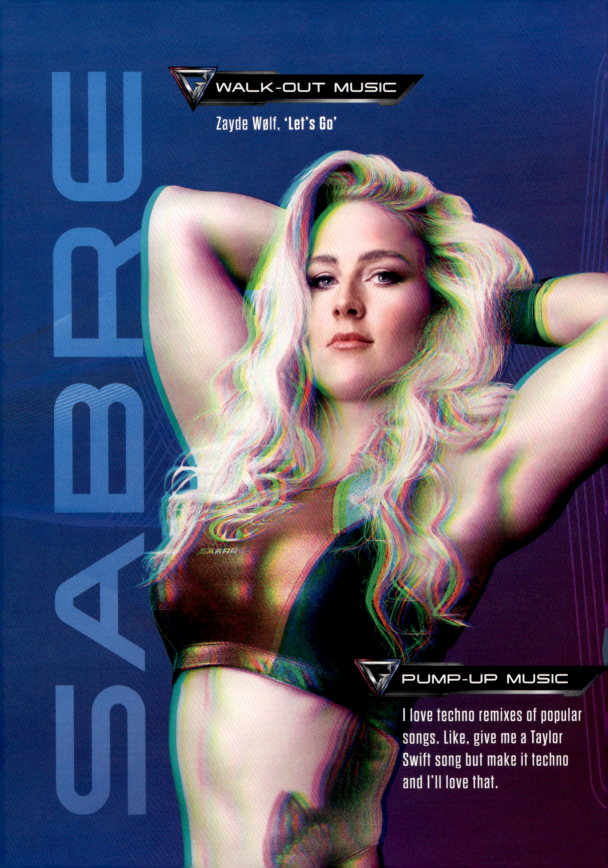

SABRE

WALK-OUT MUSIC

Zayde Wølf, 'Let's Go'

PUMP-UP MUSIC

I love techno remixes of popular songs. Like, give me a Taylor Swift song but make it techno and I'll love that.

STEEL

WALK-OUT MUSIC

Tinie Tempah, 'Pass Out'

PUMP-UP MUSIC

'Forefather' by Benga and Kano — it's always been my favourite get-hype tune. I listen to it before a big lift, or any competitions, and now I listen to it all the time for *Gladiators*.

MEET THE GLADIATOR

STATS

HEIGHT: **5 ft 5 in***

BICEP: **29.5cm**

KEY SKILL: **Explosive power**

'I might look small and sweet, but don't be fooled: I hit hard.'

*(and a half)

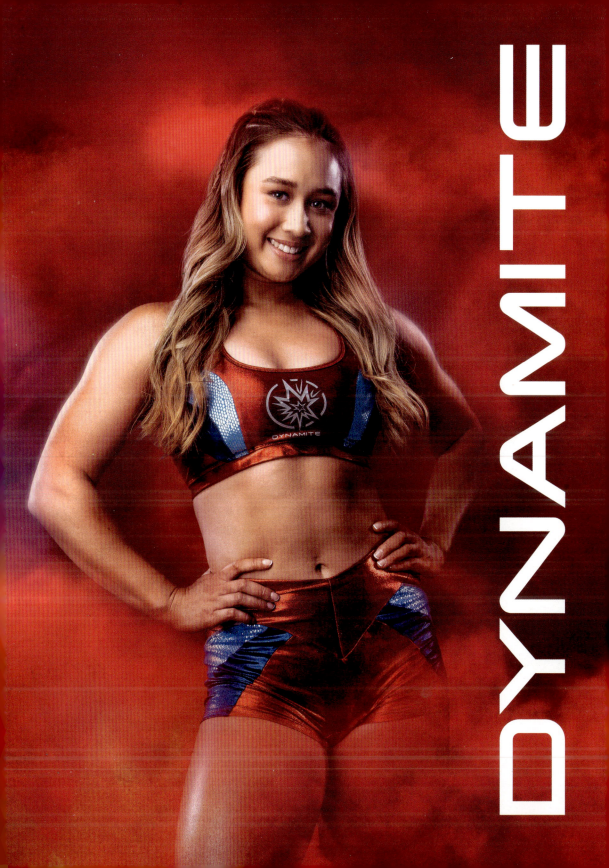

DYNAMITE

INTRODUCING DYNAMITE

DID YOU KNOW?

Dynamite's first ever *Gladiators* appearance took place one hour after finishing a three-hour university exam.

MAXIMUM CLEAN & JERK

110kg

(heavier than twenty average bowling balls)

MAXIMUM SQUAT

145kg

(the same weight as five adult Labrador dogs)

The youngest of all the Gladiators, Dynamite might look like the easiest to defeat. But don't be fooled, because she is the real deal.

Dynamite is not only undefeated in Duel but also the best-performing female Gladiator in Hang Tough. She is also relentlessly energetic, and can often be found backstage either singing or walking about on her hands for fun.

What's most frightening about Dynamite is that, at twenty-one years old, she is only just getting started. If you think she can terrorise contenders now, just wait and see what she'll be able to do in the years to come.

ABOUT ME

The Dynamite way

To be bubbly, positive and energetic like me, you have to be passionate about anything you do, whether that's in sport or work. I'm even quite full on when I'm putting plates away at home.

My workout routine

I train CrossFit, which is a bit of everything, six days a week. In the morning, it's running, cardio machines, rowing, skiing, muscle-ups, all that jazz. And in the afternoon it's weightlifting, bodybuilding, strength training, with maybe a bit of cardio to finish. On the other day it's active recovery, which can range from a slow run to a swim to anything that isn't too strenuous.

What I eat

I have oats with Biscoff for breakfast. Lunch is usually pasta or chilli and the same thing again for dinner, with snacks in between. I live with five girls and this is a chocolate house, so after dinner we'll usually go for a walk to find a sweet treat.

My school years

I used to be really shy, although I've become a lot more confident as I've got older. At school, I was never one of those kids who would put their hand up straight away to answer a question. If I ever spoke in class it was because a teacher made me. I've always been good at sport, though, so obviously that was my favourite thing.

What I'm like in real life

I can't sit still. I'm always doing handstands or running around. I do things very fast – I feel like I'm on 10x speed all the time. You wouldn't think I had so much strength, but when I go into sport mode, my competitive side comes out. I really don't like losing things, so I just unleash it all. Think of me as a pair of trainers. You know how they can be really comfortable, but you can put them in sport mode? Yeah, that's me.

My favourite event on *Gladiators* ...

Collision is fun. You can have a laugh, because you're just swinging around kicking people off a bridge. But Duel is my favourite, even though it's the most stressful. It always makes me nervous, because it's one-on-one and everyone's looking at you, but I love it.

... and my least favourite

The Ring hasn't been great for me just because I've never done a contact sport before. But I have been doing some rugby training lately, so I'm hoping to be much better next time around.

My journey

I get underestimated quite a lot, because I'm tiny. Well, not *tiny*, but compared to the other Gladiators I'm very small and still very fresh in my sporting career. I think people look at me and just think, 'Oh cute, I'll beat her.' But then they don't. I don't know why people underestimate me; my stats speak for themselves. So for me, part of my journey has definitely been about proving a point. I may look baby-faced and sweet – but don't be fooled.

My hero

The other Gladiators. They are all so inspirational, and I love being friends with all of them. They're also really good to go to for advice. I go to a lot of the girls for sporting advice, as well as silly boyfriend stuff, things like that. They've all gone through it.

What I've learned

Being on *Gladiators* has taught me to be more confident. Before one show I had doubts about one of the events, and I was really nervous. But backstage,

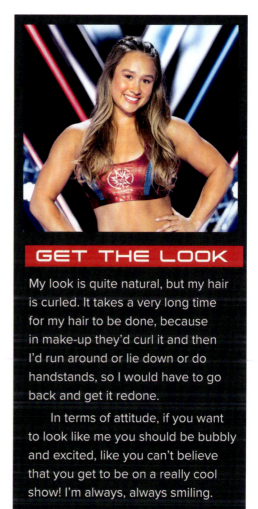

GET THE LOOK

My look is quite natural, but my hair is curled. It takes a very long time for my hair to be done, because in make-up they'd curl it and then I'd run around or lie down or do handstands, so I would have to go back and get it redone.

In terms of attitude, if you want to look like me you should be bubbly and excited, like you can't believe that you get to be on a really cool show! I'm always, always smiling.

the rest of the Gladiators were like, 'You need to stop doubting yourself. You're strong.' And from that my confidence just grew and grew. Now I know exactly who I am as a Gladiator. I know my strengths and my weaknesses, but I also know that I'm working on my weaknesses.

GAUNTLET

HOW IT WORKS

One of the most hard-fought events on the show, Gauntlet is an incredibly intimidating thing to face. Scattered along the length of a narrow, fifteen-metre gutter are several Gladiators, padded up and ready to stomp. Somehow, contenders are going to have to find the speed, strength and bravery to bash past all of them in the allotted time. If there is any event in which tempers will flare between contenders and Gladiators, it will be here. Strap in, everyone. This could get nasty.

BASICS

TIME LIMIT (HEATS):	**30** secs
(SEMIS & FINAL):	**20** secs
GLADIATORS:	**4**
CONTENDERS:	**1**
WEAPONS:	**Ram rods & pads**

SCORING

EACH ZONE CLEARED:	**2** POINTS
FOR COMPLETION:	**10** POINTS

'If there is any event in which tempers will flare, it will be here.'

HANG TOUGH

HOW IT WORKS

It's one thing to be able to swing from ring to ring like Tarzan. But Hang Tough is so much more than that. Not only will contenders need to possess the iron grip necessary to cross the rings and make it to the Gladiator's podium, but they'll also need to hold their nerve while an oncoming Gladiator tries to pull them down to the crash mats three metres below. Maybe they'll get lucky and avoid a clash. But if they aren't, and a Gladiator latches on and starts tugging with all their weight, they had better hold on for dear life.

BASICS

TIME LIMIT: **60** secs
GLADIATORS: **1**
CONTENDERS: **1**
WEAPONS: **None**

SCORING

FOR A SUCCESSFUL CROSSING: **10** POINTS
HANGING TOUGH IN RED ZONE: **5** POINTS
HANGING TOUGH IN GREY ZONE: **0** POINTS

'Contenders need to hold their nerve while an oncoming Gladiator tries to pull them down.'

THE ELIMINATOR

HOW IT WORKS

The epic, legendary final event. You won't find any Gladiators here. This is contender versus contender, and only one can win. Over this gruelling, nine-stage obstacle course, the contenders' bodies – already worn out from the previous rounds – will be tested to their limits in multiple ways. The hurdles look easy, but getting to the ground and back up again is deceptively hard. Approach the rope climb wrong and contenders will lose valuable time and strength. Fail to take the overhead ladder and trapeze seriously and they will fall. There's a cargo net climb designed to sap every ounce of their energy, and then an exhilarating zipwire ride leading to a balance beam that needs to be conquered while breathless. And then, the ultimate *Gladiators* test. The Travelator is a blazingly fast treadmill running against contenders at a 25-degree angle. They'll need explosive speed to beat it. They'll need total focus. If anyone has it in them to reach the top, take on the final rope swing and burst through the paper barrier before their opponent, they'll truly deserve their victory.

BASICS

TIME LIMIT: **To completion**
GLADIATORS: **0**
CONTENDERS: **2**
WEAPONS: **None**

SCORING

WINNER TAKES ALL

'This is contender versus contender, and only one can win.'

RULES

The contender with the most points from the previous events receives a head start, dependent on the point difference with their opponent.

Each point gained from earlier rounds is worth a half a second head start.

SKILLS

SPEED: ▽ ▽ ▽ ▽ ▽

STRENGTH: ▽ ▽ ▽ ▽ ▽

AGILITY: ▽ ▽ ▽ ▽ ▽

BRAVERY: ▽ ▽ ▽ ▽ ▽

DO IT YOURSELF

So, you watched *Gladiators* and now you want to compete in some of the events. Well, first of all, steady on! *Gladiators* is a show about trained professionals who are covered from head to toe in safety equipment and have teams of medics surrounding them in case things go wrong. This is not the sort of thing you can easily recreate at home.

But the good news is that you can still safely recreate the spirit of some of the iconic events. Here are some suggestions.

Duel

Please don't try to knock each other off three-metre-high podiums by thumping each other in the head with pugil sticks,

because that's for trained Gladiators only. But there are still ways to practise the most famous event on the show. Draw a circle around you and try to stand your ground while your friends try to push you out of it. This will require a solid centre of gravity and an extremely strong core, two things that will definitely help you when you get the call to try the event for real. No hitting, no head blows, just sheer resistance.

The Ring

On *Gladiators*, The Ring is a bruising contact game where Gladiators tackle contenders hard. But the heart of the event is about speed and agility: it's all about being able to run fast and change direction as quickly as possible. Why not try playing

a non-contact version of The Ring using Touch Rugby rules? Put a pile of jumpers in the middle of a field. Your job is to run to it and touch it without your opponent tagging you first. No tackles or grabbing!

The Wall

As many of the Gladiators themselves have said, the only way to train for The Wall is to go climbing. Forget chasing or being chased – the goal of this event is to clamber up a vertical surface as quickly as you possibly can. And this is something you can learn to do on a commercial climbing wall. Perhaps your local leisure centre has one, where you'll wear a helmet and be clipped into a harness that will stop you falling if you make a mistake. These walls can be scary at first, but remember the *Gladiators* mindset: focus hard and never give up!

Hang Tough

Like Lee Phillips said earlier, the main challenge of Hang Tough is being able to hold your own body weight for as long as you can. If you want to test this out with your friends, just jump up and grab an overhead ladder (you can often find them in parks) and hang on to it for dear life. Don't worry about swinging from bar to bar, or having someone try to pull you down from

them. Just grab the bars and time each other while you cling on for as long as you possibly can. Whoever stays up there the longest wins!

The Edge

Fury's dad helped her prepare for The Edge by building her a home version of the event. 'It wasn't up high or anything,' she says, 'But he laid out the grid of it on the floor to help me get used to the movements.' Fury's trick was to forget the height and just concentrate on the criss-cross lattice of the event itself. Set something similar up with chalk or cones and try to get past each other without being tagged.

The Eliminator

First the bad news: there is no safe way for you to replicate The Eliminator in full without actually signing up for *Gladiators*. But there are still elements you can mimic at home. If you have benches, jump over and crawl under them. If you see a playground with a cargo net, try to climb it as quickly as you can. Then there's the balance beam: draw a line on the ground and try to teeter along it without falling off. Double points if you can do it while you're out of breath. If you want to make it more like the TV event, punch through a bit of toilet paper when you're done. You're a champion!

MEET THE GLADIATOR

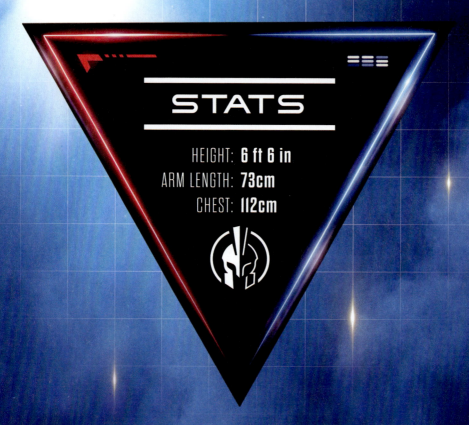

STATS

HEIGHT: **6 ft 6 in**
ARM LENGTH: **73cm**
CHEST: **112cm**

'Bring it on! Good luck going against me,
I have the height, strength and
power of the gods.'

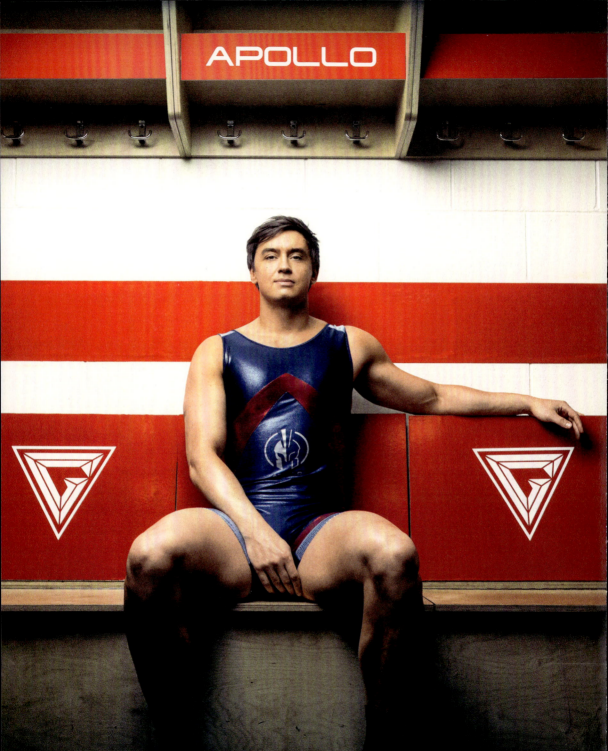

APOLLO

INTRODUCING APOLLO

DID YOU KNOW?

Apollo once ended a round of Powerball by dumping his competitor into a bin.

FASTEST 100 METRES

11 seconds
(this is very fast for a big guy)

MAXIMUM BENCH PRESS

150kg
(the same weight as two washing machines)

Few Gladiators wear their confidence as openly on their sleeve as Apollo. A former rugby player turned star of America's National Football League (NFL), he's made a career of contact sport, and he wears this like a badge of honour.

In *Gladiators* 2024 he competed in The Edge five times, and only came off it once, plus he currently holds the record for the quickest takedown in that event. Not only that, but he's faced more Powerball competitors than any other male Gladiator. As such, he is completely aware of his ability, and ready to take down anyone who disagrees.

ABOUT ME

The Apollo way

I'm ambitious, positive, always striving for greatness. It's all about aspiration and inspiration for me.

My workout routine

Five days of training, two sessions a day. We're talking speed work, weights, fitness conditioning, cardio. Before *Gladiators* I had never done any rock climbing, so now I do that too. I got a couple of wins on The Wall, so it's working.

What I eat

Nutrition is definitely one thing that I've got to be focused on, especially as a bigger guy doing a lot of exercise. It takes a lot of calories to fuel me. I probably consume around 4,000 calories a day, which means four or five meals. Breakfast is always six eggs, two slices of toast and porridge with berries. I'm not at the point where I'm fed up of eating so much, but I've definitely been there before.

Growing up

I loved going into school, mostly because I just loved hanging out with my mates. I was a good student, but I did a lot of daydreaming, looking out the window at the sports fields. I enjoyed school. I could play with my mates. I could flirt with the girls. And I could play a lot of sports. It was a great time.

What I'm like in real life

In my sporting career, I switched sports from rugby to American football, even though I'd never even been to an American football match before. It's probably the most competitive sports league in the world. There are 70,000 college kids that come through every year, who all want to play in the NFL. So, for me to end up there was one of those things that you can only dream of. The opportunity gave me a chance to redefine not only who I was as an athlete, but also who I was as a human and how I wanted to attack life.

My favourite event on *Gladiators* ...

I'm perfect for Powerball as I love smashing contenders, being really physical — all the rough, tough stuff.

... and my least favourite

There aren't any I don't like, because *Gladiators* is ultimately a big kids'

playground. We've got a climbing wall; we've got a trapeze. People would pay good money to do that stuff. Some of the others said they don't like Gauntlet? That's because they're not me, buddy. Guys running straight at you, and you've got a licence to knock ten bells out of them? What a dream.

My journey

The NFL is a very brutal place. The sport is very hard to get into, but it's even harder to stay in. I would sometimes go to breakfast with a guy, and by lunchtime there'd already be someone new sitting in his spot. When you join a rugby team, you're automatically given thirty mates. Whereas in an American football team, 70 per cent of the squad changes every year. So you don't build those really close friendships with people. It was an amazing experience, but I don't think there's a more brutal, more competitive sporting environment than that.

GET THE LOOK

You can't ignore the floppy hair. Think Harry Styles, but massive and tough. Obviously it's important to have loads of confidence, too: the way you walk and the way you talk is probably more important than a hairstyle! So chin up and chest out. Those who think they can and those that think they can't, are both usually right.

My hero

You want to talk about toughness? Let's talk about my mum. She's the toughest person I know. She's worked in the NHS for thirty-five years, and she's only missed one day through sickness. She's kept going through bad health, through tiredness, night shifts, the lot. She's definitely a hero and inspiration, I'd say.

What I've learned

Gladiators has made me realise how much I love the buzz of playing in front of a crowd. If you could bottle that feeling and sell it, you'd be very rich. It's one of those things that 99 per cent of all humans will never have the chance to experience. So to be able to do that, I just feel very, very lucky.

LOCKER-ROOM SECRETS

Watch any episode of *Gladiators*, and you'll quickly realise that the locker room is a special place. It isn't just where the Gladiators prepare for the show and flex their enormous biceps in front of each other – it's where they get to celebrate victories and commiserate defeats. The locker room is a place where they can escape the noise and excitement of the arena and connect with each other as competitors and people.

For viewers, the glimpses we get into the locker room offer a fascinating peek behind the curtain – a chance for us to see the Gladiators as athletes rather than superheroes. But for the Gladiators themselves, it's one of the most important spaces they have. Let's hear what they have to say about it.

Team support

Although the Gladiators bonded into a tightly knit group from day one, having a communal area where they can boost each other has certainly helped. 'The locker room is a place where we can show our raw emotion after the events,' explains Electro. 'But that means it's also the place where we get to support each other as a team. People bond a lot in there. The locker room is probably where we all discovered how strong we could be as a collective.'

'We're always there for each other, through victory or loss,' adds Steel. 'We've got each other's backs in the locker room, because we're all going through the same thing, and we all want the same thing. We're just

'The locker room is a place where we can show our raw emotion after the events.'

ELECTRO

a big, tight family that sticks together no matter what happens. Wins, losses, injuries. No one goes into anything alone, so it's great to have a place where we can all be together.'

'We're all very motivating people,' adds Diamond. 'When one of us gets ready for an event, we're all hyping them up and giving out positivity. It's awesome!'

The mood of the room

But the atmosphere of the Gladiators' locker room can also change as the day goes on. Depending on what happens to be taking place inside the arena, the mood can shift throughout the day. 'Sometimes it's really high in energy, and everyone's dancing and ready to go out,' says Fury. 'But then other times it can get really quiet, because everyone's so focused. Sometimes you need a moment of quiet before going into the next event. A lot of the mood depends on what's just happened in the arena. If someone's had a good game, everyone's congratulating them. But if it goes badly, we have to pick them up a bit and help them get ready for the next job. It's never the same. There's always such a variety.'

Inevitably, Legend has a slightly different take on the matter. 'I've only ever seen the locker room euphoric, but that's only because I'm there,' he boasts, in true

Legend style. 'I just transform the space. People say, "Wow, when you're here, it's so much better." And it makes me feel bad, because I'm just a man and I can't spend an equal amount of time with everyone. Imagine if you and your friends went to a retreat with Mahatma Gandhi and Martin Luther King, and your friends got to spend more time with them than you did. You'd be furious. That's what it's like for the other Gladiators when they don't get enough Legend time.'

A place to relax ...

'Sometimes we have a couple of hours between events,' explains Bionic. 'When that happens, it's important to chill out as much as you can. You can't see them onscreen, but we have a few massive beanbags in the locker room, so I'll usually

> 'It's all calm and fun, right until the event is about to begin. Then you start to get hyped up.'
> GIANT

just go over to one of them and crash until it's time to dial in for the next event.'

'It's quite a chilled-out place for the most part,' agrees Giant. 'Sometimes we'll play games together to pass the time, but that's usually down to Nitro. He comes to us with these brainteasers that he loves. One of them is called "In a Land...", where you have to work out the rules of the game as he's explaining it to you. He's a proper games master, that one. So it's all calm and fun, right until the event is about to begin. Then you start to get hyped up.'

... or run around

Obviously, some Gladiators relax more than others. 'I can't really sit still,' admits Dynamite. 'So I'm like, "We have to do something!" Sometimes I'll be in there doing handstands, or just running around like a child. I'll do tackling practice on the beanbags, too, if Bionic isn't lying on them! Or karaoke ... Fire and I love to belt out karaoke first thing in the morning. Like, really early in the morning. So early! Gotta wake everyone up somehow, right? Gotta keep them young.'

Sizing up the opposition

A lot has been said about the Gladiators' approach to sportsmanship. However, they are also professional athletes, and as such they want to use every opportunity to give themselves the edge over their opponents. And this means that sometimes the locker room transforms into a place where they can all get together and strategise about how to take the contenders down.

'We have a TV in there, so we can see the events as they're happening,' reveals Comet. 'So obviously we watch them and discuss them with each other – and we tend to be very honest and open! We assess each other's performances and notice things that worked well, as well as mention things that annoyed us, including things the contenders did. Sometimes the screen will show us something we missed during the event. Then everyone is like, "Did you see that? Did you see what she did?" And then we all get pumped up about it, like, "Right, it's game time!"'

'The time we have to analyse the contenders' performances is important,' adds Electro. 'Obviously, we all want to get better as the series goes on, so we learn from each other's techniques and collect data about the contenders, by watching their performance and sharing it with each other. We're watching their skills and their weaknesses and their temperament, and we use it to our advantage in the events. We're a team, after all, and that's what teams do.'

MEET THE GLADIATOR

STATS

HEIGHT: **5 ft 7 in**
BICEP: **31cm**
LOVES: **Heights**

'You can run …
but I will always catch my prey!'

INTRODUCING SABRE

DID YOU KNOW?

Sabre's favourite way to intimidate the contenders is to growl at them.

MAXIMUM BACK SQUAT

145kg

(heavier than two adult male leopards)

MAXIMUM NUMBER OF UNBROKEN HANDSTAND PUSH-UPS

61

(a lot)

Fierce and athletic, there's an unpredictability to Sabre's performance that is thrilling to watch.

Very few Gladiators can stare down contenders like Sabre. When she sets her mind on defeating them, almost nothing can stop her. They are her prey, and she is determined to hunt them.

But this just underlines Sabre's undying dedication when it comes to the task at hand. Nobody quite attacks their role on *Gladiators* like Sabre, and you just have to look at her legions of fans for proof of how people relate to her incredible commitment.

ABOUT ME

The Sabre way

I'm playful but don't mess with me. I'm fun but strong, powerful and fierce.

My workout routine

I train almost every day. I spend time on the rings, climbing and tackling people to the ground, as well as fifteen hours of CrossFit a week, and Olympic weightlifting, and running, and swimming. I love to ride bikes, wakeboard and paddleboard. Oh, and I also walk my dog.

What I eat

Everything. Due to my intensive training I eat 3,000 calories a day, and 150 grams of protein. Generally, I have a fairly low-fat diet. The remaining calories come from carbohydrates, such as rice, grains, porridge and bagels. And then one day a week I have a totally vegetarian day, just because it encourages me to eat all of my beets, legumes, salad and vegetables. I'm a hungry girl.

Growing up

I was a tomboy. I rode horses from the age of four, so as a kid I was riding all the time. At school I was a bit of a loser. I didn't have a big group of friends, and I wasn't much of an academic either. It wasn't until I left school and went to college that I grew to love learning.

What I'm like in real life

I've been full-time in sport for ten years, and competitive to an elite standard for about five or six. In order to compete internationally, you have to be serious about it and put in many hours of work. What I love about CrossFit is that you have to be very aware of yourself and know yourself so well, so that you can strategise about the best way to push yourself to your limit.

My favourite event on *Gladiators* …

One of my strengths is my versatility, so I enjoy all the events. But I do really like the thrill of The Edge. It's really scary up there, and I like the fact that the contender I'm up there with is really scared too. I run on adrenaline, so I like that feeling.

… and my least favourite

I didn't have the best time on Gauntlet. In one episode I dropped my pads and took on a contender without them. And that pretty much sums up my competitive spirit. Those pads are more trouble than they're worth. I'd prefer to use boxing gloves. Plus the contender was trash-talking me, so I'm not sorry.

My journey

At university, I stopped riding horses. I became overweight, and very inactive. I was really unhappy. But a couple of boys at uni were doing this thing called CrossFit, so I decided to give it a go. It was awful at first – it literally made me feel sick to push myself so hard. But after about six months, I realised how powerful the human body is. Sport is a place where women are allowed to be unapologetically athletic, and it allowed me to be unapologetic as well. Every single great person has overcome adversity at one point or another, because adversity sharpens your focus.

My hero

My mum – she was a sergeant in the Army. If my goal was to grow up to be a strong, independent, driven, inspirational female in terms of both work ethic and morals, my mum's values and vision were impeccable guides for me. I couldn't have asked for a better role model.

What I've learned

I've learned that I'm a show-off. It's so exhilarating to perform in front of a

GET THE LOOK

Well, you need to have an absolutely massive sweep of wild mane-like hair. You need to be constantly prowling round, ready to pounce, and take absolutely zero rubbish from anyone. One of my entrance moves is a hip-pop that came about by accident. During rehearsals I was coming down the stairs, and the cameraman accidentally came too close. So I just hip-popped him out of the way, and now that move has somehow become my signature.

crowd! I've also discovered that I'm a real team person. I enjoy feeling like I belong in the Gladiator family. If one of the others does well, I feel genuine joy. I've made very intense friendships with people I'd never met before, and I care deeply about them.

MEET BRADLEY & BARNEY

Gladiators wouldn't be Gladiators without its presenters. A show this big needs a ringmaster – and this time around we've got two from the same family! Gladiators is hosted by the real-life father-and-son pairing of Bradley and Barney Walsh.

Award-winning actor and presenter Bradley Walsh has been a household name for decades. While much-loved as the host of *Blankety Blank*, *The Chase* and *Beat the Chasers*, he has also starred in *Doctor Who* and released two albums.

Barney Walsh continues to shine on Saturday-night TV as he stars in continuing drama *Casualty*. Barney has had acting roles in many projects including Guy Ritchie's feature film *King Arthur: Legend of the Sword*. Alongside his impressive acting career, Barney is an absolute thrill-seeker and loves challenging his dad in their travelogue series *Bradley Walsh & Son: Breaking Dad*.

Bradley and Barney are the perfect hosts for a show like *Gladiators*. They're funny, they're experienced, and they've got each other's backs when some of the cheekier Gladiators start mucking around. Let's learn more about our intrepid hosts.

BRADLEY

What's it like filming *Gladiators*?
It's great! The Gladiators and contenders are all incredible to watch, and the audience is out of this world. I mean, the atmosphere is electric. It's like being at a concert rather than a TV show!

We film the TV series, but we also have a live show going on at the same time, with Stuart Holdham and two DJs from a local radio station, Mylo and Rosie, keeping the audience entertained. They work brilliantly together, and it feels like a really special event.

What did you think of the set when you saw it for the first time in the arena?
It was mesmerising. The production team kept the set from us for quite some time. The day before we were going to rehearse, Barney and I walked into the training session and saw the Gladiators training on the equipment. We thought, 'This is absolutely amazing!'

'I'd like to think I'd be good at Duel, but if I was face to face with Giant, I don't think I'd win that!'
BARNEY

Did you have to put any of the Gladiators in their place?

No, they were so respectful, apart from Viper and Legend! Viper hardly spoke, and Legend spoke too much! At one point Legend picked Barney up and threw him onto the mat, then he took my microphone and threw it. It can be hard work dealing with them sometimes, it really can, but it was all in good fun and in general they are wonderful to work with.

BARNEY

Was filming *Gladiators* what you expected?

I didn't expect that atmosphere! That's a vivid memory for me, walking out for the first time, because 3,000 people is a lot. I mean it sounds like a massive number, but you can't really imagine it until you walk out there. You've got everyone surrounding you in that big round arena, all the lights going off, all the cannons, and everyone screaming and cheering. It's spectacular.

What is your favourite event?

I really love The Edge and how it starts. It's cool when the whole arena goes dark and then lights up, as it gets higher and higher. When you're standing there, it's magnificent. And I don't have a fear of heights, so I think I'd be pretty good at it.

Which Gladiator would you least like to go up against?

I like to think I'd be good at Duel, but if I was face to face with Giant, I don't think I'd win that! And I wouldn't want to go up against Nitro in anything that required a lot of speed, either. He would be tough to beat on The Wall because he's very quick. But they are all tough. They're Gladiators!